THE INSPIRED CHOICE

Chronicles: Built to Give

Volume 3

Caroline Biesalski

The Inspired Choice

Chronicles Built to Give

Caroline Biesalski

Foreword by Dr. Peggy McColl

Bibliografische Information der Deutschen Nationalbibliothek:
Die Deutsche Nationalbibliothek verzeichnet diese Publikation
in der Deutschen Nationalbibliografie; detaillierte
bibliografische Daten sind im Internet über http://dnb.dnb.de
abrufbar.

Verlag: BoD · Books on Demand GmbH, Überseering 33,
22297 Hamburg, bod@bod.de

Druck: Libri Plureos GmbH, Friedensallee 273, 22763 Hamburg

ISBN: 978-3-8192-2708-0

CONTENTS

I

In a world filled with noise, distraction, and a never-ending pursuit of "more," it is both rare and refreshing to discover a book that speaks to the heart of what truly matters: contribution. *The Inspired Choice Chronicles: Built to Give* is not only a timely message—it's a necessary one. As someone who has spent nearly five decades guiding individuals to step into their power, align with purpose, and realize their dreams, I've learned this: the most meaningful success is never about accumulation. It's about *amplification*. It's about discovering who you are, elevating your own life, and then using that power to uplift others. That is the essence of this book. That is the essence of *giving*. When I sat down with Caroline Biesalski to talk about what inspires me, our conversation naturally centered around service—how one person's choice to follow their calling can become a catalyst for transformation, not only in their own life but in the lives of countless others. This is what Caroline lives and breathes. It is what *The Inspired Choice* stands for. Caroline doesn't just interview people—she connects with them. She doesn't just curate stories—she *amplifies* them. And in this volume, she has woven together a powerful tapestry of voices, experiences, and perspectives that all share one common thread: the power of giving as a vehicle for personal and collective evolution. Having authored 23 books myself, each one written with the intention to help someone shift, grow, and awaken, I can say with full confidence that this book belongs in your hands. It belongs in libraries, in nonprofits, in homes, in boardrooms. Why? Because it speaks to the truth we all sense deep down: We are *meant* to live lives of impact. One of the most beautiful things about being of service—whether through writing, coaching, mentoring, or simply holding space—is how it transforms *us* in the process. I shared this with Caroline during our conversation: every time I write a book, I evolve. I change. Not because I set out to, but because creation is a mirror. Giving is a mirror. It reflects our own growth, our own willingness to go deeper. This book will do the same for you. As you turn each page, you will meet individuals who chose to serve rather than stay silent. Who chose contribution over comfort. Who chose to build businesses, movements, and missions that don't just generate income—but *create meaning*. These are people who answered the call to give, and in doing so, found a life richer than they imagined. And make no mistake, this is not a book just for people in the nonprofit space. It's for anyone who has ever felt that tug—that soul whisper— that says, "There's something more I'm here to do." It's for entrepreneurs, creatives, community builders, and changemakers. It's for anyone ready to shift from hustle to heart, from success to significance. Caroline's brilliance lies not only in the questions she asks, but in the spaces she creates. *The Inspired Choice Chronicles* is more than a series—it's a movement. A movement toward remembering that your purpose is not a destination; it's a decision. And giving is the most powerful decision you can make.

To give is to lead.
To give is to heal.
To give is to rise.

As you read the stories within this book, I invite you to reflect on your own journey. Ask yourself: *Where can I give more? Where can I serve deeper? Where can I live more fully aligned with who I truly am?* If you do, you may just find that the impact you make on others becomes the very thing that transforms you. Thank you, Caroline, for this inspired body of work. Thank you to every contributor who chose to say yes. And thank you, dear reader, for having the courage to make your own inspired choice.

With love and gratitude,
Dr. Peggy McColl
New York Times Bestselling Author & Founder

www.peggymccoll.com

THE CALL TO GIVE

When you hear the word "giving," you might first think of charity, donations, or volunteer work. But at its core, giving is much bigger than that. Giving is a mindset—a decision to live, lead, and build businesses in a way that leaves the world better than we found it. In *The Inspired Choice Chronicles: Built to Give*, we explore the idea that building a life or a company is not just about achieving personal success; it's about creating value beyond ourselves. It's about choosing to act with courage, compassion, and commitment, even when the world urges us to focus only on what we gain. Each story in this book is a living example of what happens when individuals and entrepreneurs choose to lead with purpose. From breakthrough moments to bold decisions, our featured changemakers show that giving is not something reserved for "someday." It is part of how we build today—and it shapes the legacy we leave behind. This is not about perfection. It's not about grand gestures. It's about everyday inspired choices: choosing to believe in someone's potential, choosing to act when it's easier to stay comfortable, choosing to create solutions that serve not only the bottom line but the greater good.

In these pages, you'll meet individuals who turned their defining moments into movements. You'll see how service, mentorship, education, and contribution can become powerful strategies for business and life. And you'll find inspiration and actionable insights to start building your own journey of impact, no matter where you are today. The world needs more leaders who are **built to give**—who understand that true success is measured not just by what we achieve, but by what we create for others.

You are one of those leaders.
Welcome to the Inspired Choice Chronicles.

Welcome to *Built to Give*.

1. REDEFINING SUCCESS: WHY GIVING BACK IS THE REAL ROI

Success.
For much of our lives, we're taught that success looks a certain way: titles on a business card, trophies on the shelf, zeros on a paycheck. We chase external measures, believing they will fill the internal spaces we hope to satisfy—significance, security, satisfaction. But the deeper truth is this: lasting fulfillment doesn't come from what we accumulate. It comes from what we contribute. When we give, we tap into the most authentic version of ourselves. We create meaning not just for ourselves, but for others. And in doing so, we experience the real return on investment—the growth of human potential, the strengthening of communities, and the shaping of a legacy that endures beyond our personal achievements. Many of the changemakers you'll meet in this book came to this realization at a critical moment in their journey. Some reached material success and found it hollow. Others recognized early on that climbing ladders wasn't enough—they needed to build bridges too. Their paths diverged from the traditional, and by embracing a giving mindset, they not only enriched the lives of others—they amplified their own success in ways they hadn't imagined. Giving back is not an afterthought to success. It's the engine of it. Businesses that center service and contribution at their core build stronger brands, deeper loyalty, and cultures of resilience. Leaders who mentor, coach, and empower their teams create organizations that thrive beyond any one person's effort. In today's world, impact is a currency. People want to work for, buy from, and partner with organizations and individuals who stand for something greater than themselves. And yet, embracing giving as part of your success model isn't just good strategy—it's good living. It brings a sense of connectedness in an often fragmented world. It gives meaning to the long hours and challenges, anchoring our efforts in something that matters.

Importantly, giving back doesn't have to mean abandoning ambition. In fact, the two fuel each other. The more you grow, the more you have to give. The more you give, the more authentic your growth becomes. Imagine redefining success not as "what did I win?" but as "who did I help rise?" Not as "what did I achieve?" but "what did we build together?" Not as "what legacy did I leave?" but "what future did I help create?" Success becomes less about accumulation and more about multiplication. Every skill you sharpen, every dollar you earn, every opportunity you seize becomes a resource to expand your impact. This redefinition doesn't happen overnight. It happens in the choices you make each day:

- Choosing to mentor a young entrepreneur instead of seeing them as competition.
- Choosing to design products that solve real problems, not just create profit.
- Choosing to invest time into building relationships, not just transactions.
- Choosing to lead with empathy, not just efficiency.

In the coming chapters, you'll see example after example of leaders who made these choices—and how it transformed not only their work but their lives.

You have the power to redefine success on your own terms. You have the power to measure ROI not just in returns to yourself but in returns to the world around you.

The greatest achievement isn't what you can accumulate for yourself.
It's what you inspire, create, and ignite in others.

That's the real return on investment.
And it's waiting for you to claim it.

2. FROM HUSTLE TO HEART: THE PURPOSE-DRIVEN PIVOT

The hustle is celebrated. Our culture glorifies it—late nights, early mornings, packed schedules, endless to-do lists. Hustling becomes a badge of honor, a sign that you're serious, ambitious, committed. And for a time, it works. It gets you moving. It teaches discipline. It pushes you to achieve things you once thought impossible. But hustle alone isn't sustainable. Left unchecked, it leads to burnout, emptiness, and the haunting question: *Is this all there is?* The pivotal realization— the one that every truly impactful leader eventually encounters—is this: hustle can build a career, but heart builds a legacy. The purpose-driven pivot isn't about abandoning ambition. It's about aligning it with meaning. It's about asking: *What am I hustling for? Who am I serving? What bigger story am I part of?* When your energy is fueled not just by personal goals but by purpose, you unlock a different kind of power. Your work becomes a mission, not just a job. Your growth becomes an offering, not just an accolade. Your days become opportunities to make a difference, not just to move the needle. The changemakers featured in this book made this pivot. For some, it came through a personal loss that reoriented their priorities. For others, it emerged from a growing sense of disillusionment with the traditional measures of success. Each one chose to move from **hustling for themselves** to **working from a place of service**—and in doing so, they found greater fulfillment, deeper resilience, and broader impact. Making the shift from hustle to heart doesn't mean you stop working hard. It means you work harder *for something bigger than yourself.*

It means:

- You build businesses that solve meaningful problems, not just chase market trends.

- You create spaces where others can grow, not just protect your own position.
- You celebrate not just what you've achieved, but what you've helped others achieve.

The pivot starts inside. It begins when you quiet the noise long enough to ask yourself:

- What really matters to me?
- What kind of legacy do I want to leave?
- How do I want people to feel because I existed?

Purpose redefines productivity. You stop measuring your days by how many tasks you completed and start measuring them by how much value you created. You stop chasing endless growth and start cultivating sustainable, meaningful impact. The irony is, when you lead with heart, the results often exceed what hustle alone could have delivered. People are drawn to authenticity. They are moved by leaders who care. They are loyal to missions that matter. Heart-based leadership doesn't dilute success—it accelerates it. Of course, making the pivot isn't always easy. It often means saying no to opportunities that don't align with your deeper values. It may require stepping away from familiar but hollow paths. It demands the courage to choose significance over short-term wins.

But the rewards are profound:

- A business that becomes a force for good.
- A career that aligns with your true calling.
- A life that feels not just full, but fulfilling.

Every journey to lasting impact begins with a decision: **Am I willing to build from heart, not just from hustle?**

You don't have to give up your ambition. You don't have to stop striving for excellence. But when you root those drives in service, when you centre them around purpose, you create success that not only elevates you—it uplifts everyone around you. Hustle will get you started. Heart will take you where you're truly meant to go.

3. THE RIPPLE-EFFECT: ONE LIFE, ONE CHOICE, MANY IMPACTED

We often underestimate the power of a single choice. We tell ourselves that our actions are too small, our resources too limited, our reach too short. But in truth, every decision we make sends ripples outward—touching lives we may never meet, shaping futures we cannot even imagine. One inspired choice can start a chain reaction that alters communities, industries, and generations to come. One moment of courage, generosity, or vision can be the seed that grows into a movement. This is the ripple effect: the quiet but powerful reality that every life, and every choice within that life, matters. Think of the teachers who believe in a struggling student, changing the course of that child's future. Think of the entrepreneurs who take a chance on a bold idea, opening doors for jobs, innovation, and community transformation. Think of the mentors who give their time freely, sparking confidence in the next generation of leaders. Their acts were not broadcast on global stages. They were choices made in real life, with real stakes—and they rippled outward, creating change far beyond the original moment. When you live with awareness of the ripple effect, you approach your decisions differently. You realize that the smallest actions—a kind word, a shared resource, a willingness to listen—have impact. You stop waiting for the "perfect" moment to make a difference and start creating difference wherever you are, right now. Giving is one of the most powerful forms of ripple-making. When you give—whether it is time, expertise, resources, or encouragement—you are not simply transferring something from yourself to someone else. You are investing in a chain of impact. You are empowering others to rise, to grow, to give back in their own right. Your one act of giving multiplies as it moves forward, creating waves of possibility. In business, this principle is just as powerful. Companies that prioritize giving—whether through service, mentorship, innovation, or philanthropy—build cultures of impact. They attract people who want to do meaningful work. They foster loyalty, creativity, and resilience. They leave legacies that are measured not just in profits, but in the lives they uplift. In nonprofit work, ripple effects are the heartbeat of every mission. You feed one person, and you nourish a family. You educate one student, and you uplift a community. You heal one heart, and you strengthen countless others. Every act of service echoes. Importantly, the ripple effect also reminds us that we may never see the full fruits of our labor. Sometimes the results of our giving are immediate and visible. Other times, they are quiet, slow-growing, hidden from view. But they are no less real. Trust that the seeds you plant matter, even if you never witness the harvest. Your life is already creating ripples. Every conversation you have, every relationship you nurture, every value you embody sends energy outward. The question is not whether you will create impact. The question is what kind of impact you choose to create. You do not have to be famous. You do not have to be wealthy. You simply have to be willing. Willing to believe that your choices matter. Willing to act even when the outcome is uncertain. Willing to trust that your life, lived with purpose, will echo beyond your own lifetime.

You have incredible power right now. In the next conversation you have. In the next decision you make. In the next opportunity you seize or create. Choose wisely. Choose generously. Choose to be a force for good.

Because when you do, you are not just changing your own life. You are creating ripples that will move through others, through communities, through the world.

One life. One choice. Many impacted.
The ripple starts with you.

4. GIVING IN ACTION: MEET EXTRAORDINARY GUESTS

Every journey has defining moments, and my podcasting path has been no exception. In this third volume of *The Inspired Choice Chronicles*, I've had the honor of speaking with extraordinary guests—purpose-driven entrepreneurs, nonprofit founders, impact leaders, and bold visionaries—who are not only building meaningful legacies, but doing so through the lens of giving.

Some episodes stand out as turning points, capturing what it means to lead with heart and to serve with purpose. I am especially proud to present this chapter, which highlights guests who embody generosity, resilience, and the spirit of contribution. These conversations go far beyond interviews— they are powerful reflections of courage, values, and the desire to leave the world better than we found it.

Volume 3 is rooted in the belief that we are all *built to give*. The Inspired Choice podcast has always been a space for transformation—where ideas become action and inspired choices become movements. In this chapter, you'll find glimpses of defining moments: stories of mission, alignment, reinvention, and impact. I hope these voices remind you that one person can make a difference—and one choice can change everything.

To hear more from these inspiring guests, tune in to *The Inspired Choice* podcast on Spotify, Apple Podcasts, Deezer, Audible, Amazon Music, and other major platforms. Full video interviews are also available on YouTube.

For the easiest access, visit https://www.podcast.inspiredchoice.today and search for the guest's name. Let their journeys inspire your own.

4.1 Scott Cutlan – The Summit Within

There are moments in life when everything appears to be in place—career success, family joy, financial stability—yet something deep inside whispers: there's more. For Scott Cutlan, that whisper became a call, and that call led to one of the most extraordinary transformations a human being can choose: the journey from outer accomplishment to inner alignment.

When I welcomed Scott onto *The Inspired Choice* podcast, I sensed immediately that this conversation would echo far beyond the bounds of a typical interview. His presence carried the energy of someone who had climbed not just the world's highest mountains, but the steepest internal ones too.

Scott is known globally as "the more guy"—a speaker, executive coach, and elite adventurer who has summited the Seven Summits, including Mount Everest. But as he humbly shared, the mountains were never the goal. They were metaphors. Training grounds. Catalysts for something deeper.

"We all climb mountains," Scott said. "The question is—are they the right ones?"

This wisdom struck a chord. He spoke of walking life's ridgeline, where one misstep could lead to a fall—not in altitude, but in purpose. The key to navigating this edge, he believes, is alignment: with our values, our purpose, and the impact we're meant to create in the world.

Scott didn't start out as a climber. In fact, he calls himself an accidental adventurer. Growing up in a broken household, he carried an innate sense that "more" was available. Not more in the sense of possessions or prestige—but more meaning, more connection, more contribution. For a long time, he didn't know how to access it. But in 2012, while serving in underprivileged communities, that dormant desire awakened. Five years later, in 2017, despite a seemingly perfect life—career, home, family—Scott knew something was missing. And he finally asked the question that would change everything: *What's the point of this success if I'm not fulfilled?*

"I had a vision," he said, "and I believed it. So I said yes."

That yes came with bold moves. He left his job. Committed to climbing the Seven Summits. Launched a nonprofit. And funded it himself. It wasn't logical. It wasn't reasonable. But it was *right*. As Scott says in his book *Unreasonable*, "Reasonable produces average. Unreasonable creates extraordinary impact."

Each summit taught Scott something profound. Not just about resilience or leadership—but about surrender, trust, and clarity. On one climb, he received the word *commitment*. On another, *willingness*. These weren't just lessons; they became guiding principles in his life and coaching work.

Through all of it, Scott developed what he now calls the *Seven Pillars of Impact*. These aren't steps to success; they're a system to help high achievers unlock exponential growth by stepping into aligned purpose. He reminds us that more isn't about doing more. It's about being more aligned. Sometimes, it's doing *less*—but with absolute clarity.

"The best of what I have—for others. That's purpose."

In this simple sentence lies the essence of Scott's message. Leadership isn't about climbing the highest peaks for recognition. It's about elevating others with every step you take. It's about clarity in purpose, commitment in action, and courage in decision-making.

One of my favorite moments from our interview was when Scott said, "Clarity creates momentum." I could feel the truth of it in every cell. When we're unclear, we hesitate. We overthink. We second-guess. But when we're *clear*, we *move*. And that movement creates ripple effects we can't even begin to imagine.

Scott's mission is now to guide others into that clarity. Through his company, seven 7 Impact, he helps leaders and teams align with their purpose and create results that matter. Not just KPIs—but fulfillment. Legacy. Impact.

Before we closed our conversation, Scott offered one final takeaway for readers:

"Your decisions, when aligned with purpose, unlock opportunity. Fulfillment isn't a destination—it's a lifestyle. Choose it, live it, share it."

This is what *Built to Give* means. Not building for ego or status—but building something that gives back. Something that lives on through the people we've touched, the truths we've shared, and the choices we've made with intention.

Scott's life is proof that legacy isn't about climbing mountains. It's about becoming the summit others are inspired to follow.

Season 11, Episode 85, aired 3/8/2025
recorded 3/8/25, Evergreen, CO, US / Lisbon, Portugal

Connect with Scott Cutlan: https://scottcutlan.com/
LinkedIn: https://www.linkedin.com/in/scottcutlan/
Book: „Unreasonable": https://amzn.to/4lkrbDq

4.2 Jim Carlough – Lead the Way, Every Day

In this heartfelt conversation with Jim Carlough, leadership strategist, speaker, and author of *The Six Pillars of Effective Leadership*, we explored what it really takes to lead with impact—every single day. With over three decades of experience building organizations from the inside out, Jim brings timeless wisdom and a refreshing perspective: leadership isn't reserved for the chosen few. It's a skill. It's a choice. And it's a commitment to growth—for yourself and those you serve.

From the very beginning of our interview, Jim made it clear: "Leadership is 24/7. It doesn't start when you sit at your desk—it begins the moment you step out of your car." That hit home. Because in a world filled with titles and optics, Jim reminds us that real leadership is demonstrated through consistency, integrity, and example. You're always on stage—and people are watching, whether you realize it or not.

He offered a personal story: as a teen, riding his bike around town, his parents somehow always knew where he was. Why? Because people talk. People observe. And that principle carries into our adult and professional lives. Leadership is networking, visibility, and trust in motion.

Jim also challenged the common corporate misconception that "hiring the best people leads to the best outcomes." It's not enough to bring in talent. You have to lead them, inspire them, and walk alongside them. "People don't follow your title," he said. "They follow your consistency. Your behavior. Your vision."

One of the most powerful shifts in our discussion was how Jim reframes organizational change. "It's not change management," he said. "It's manage change." This nuance reflects a deeper truth: top-down mandates rarely work. Sustainable transformation happens when people are invited to participate—when they feel seen, heard, and invested. Inclusion and collaboration, not commands, drive real results.

Jim emphasized that change can be scary—because it often involves movement, uncertainty, and letting go of the familiar. But it doesn't have to be isolating. "Find a mentor," he advised. "Even if it's not your direct supervisor, find someone you admire. Ask them to walk with you. Learn from their journey." Jim himself mentors up to 20 people at a time—some for over two decades—because he believes growth is not a solo sport.

When asked about new leaders entering organizations, Jim's advice was both strategic and human: align yourself with a vision bigger than you. Lead with integrity. Be consistent. And never underestimate the value of listening.

Jim's current focus is bringing *The Six Pillars of Effective Leadership* into organizations across the country—especially to empower the next generation. What began as a 20-pillar draft was refined to the six most impactful traits. The goal now? To continue expanding this framework, while keeping it accessible and actionable for leaders at every level.

Here's what I walked away with:
Leadership isn't a title. It's a presence.
It's not about knowing all the answers. It's about asking the right questions—and listening deeply.
And above all, it's about being the kind of leader people trust… even when no one's watching.

Jim's philosophy is a gift to every organization navigating growth and change. His clarity, humility, and collaborative spirit are exactly what today's leaders—and tomorrow's—need more of.

Want to learn more about Jim or connect directly?
Visit www.jimcarlough.com or find him on LinkedIn. And if you're stepping into a leadership role—or just stepping up in your own life—this conversation is your invitation to start with integrity and lead with heart.

Because when leadership is built on trust, service, and inclusion…
That's when real transformation begins.

Season 11, Episode 79, aired 3/5/2025
recorded 3/4/25, McKinney, TX, US / Bavaria, Germany

Connect with Jim Carlough: https://www.jimcarlough.com/

LinkedIn:
https://www.linkedin.com/company/jimcarloughms/posts/?feedView=all

Book: "The Six Pillars Of Effective Leadership":
https://amzn.to/4i9L6T1

4.3 Wendy Gunn – Believe to Achieve

In this deeply moving and faith-filled conversation, Wendy Gunn shared the kind of story that stops you in your tracks—not because it's dramatic for the sake of drama, but because it's *real, transformational*, and a testimony to what's possible when purpose and perseverance collide.

Wendy, now a confident Christian entrepreneur and goal achievement mentor, wasn't always that way. In fact, she described her former self as insecure, overweight, and overwhelmed by comparison. Her early life was shaped by a deep feeling of not being enough. But it was a crisis—ovarian cancer—that began a powerful transformation in both her mindset and her mission.

Faced with a devastating diagnosis, Wendy's story could have ended there. But God had other plans. Within days, prayers from friends, family, and even strangers began pouring in. What happened next was nothing short of miraculous: the cancer, previously diagnosed as aggressive and widespread, was found to be localized and treatable. Today, Wendy has been cancer-free for over 20 years.

That trial wasn't just physical—it was spiritual and emotional. "God often uses trials to transform us," Wendy said. And from that transformation emerged an unshakable purpose: to help others believe in their God-given uniqueness, embrace their personal story, and pursue their dreams—no matter their age or past.

Her story didn't stop at healing. It was only the beginning.

After 60, Wendy began setting what she calls "big goals." She lost over 100 pounds (without exercise!), built an online business, grew a 12,000+ subscriber email list, and led her family on a dream trip to Italy. She teaches others not only how to set SMART goals—but how to believe that they can *actually* achieve them, step by step, with grace and consistency.

But what truly sets Wendy apart is her heart. Her message to everyone listening, reading, or learning from her is this: *If you have breath, you have purpose.* You're not too old. It's not too late. And no, you don't need to be perfect.

"Trials transform more than triumphs," she told me. And she's living proof.

Wendy also brought a wealth of wisdom on building loyal audiences with authenticity. Her email strategy? Speak to *one person*. Be yourself. Forget perfection. Let people feel seen, heard, and understood—and they will follow you not because you're the best at something, but because you're *you*.

Now, she's moving into a new phase of impact—hosting events, writing a new book on email list building, and launching a movement with a powerful message: **Tell your story for God's glory.**

Wendy's light is contagious. Her clarity, faith, and fierce refusal to settle for "good enough" reminds us all that success is sacred when it's aligned with service. Her courage invites us to drop comparison, trust our calling, and create—even when we're scared, even when we're imperfect.

If you're over 60 (or just human), and you think your best days are behind you, Wendy is here to lovingly challenge that belief.

You're here. You have breath.
That means your purpose isn't finished.

And as Wendy says, *"If you believe—you can achieve."*

Find Wendy's resources and mentorship at yourhomeforgod.com/10-questions.
Let her story be the spark that reminds you to tell your own.

Season 12, Episode 67, aired 4/11/2025
recorded 2/20/25 Minneapolis, MN / Bavaria, Germany

Connect with Wendy: https://www.yourhomeforgod.com/

YouTube:
https://www.youtube.com/channel/UCmMr5g_UMZ1BStDYkJP
EUyg

Book "Serving from the Heart" https://amzn.to/4iUYo6N

4.4 Paul Tembunde – Lighting the Way Forward

From the moment Paul Tembunde entered our conversation, there was a calm clarity in his voice—a deep, faith-rooted conviction that greatness lies within each of us, just waiting for the spark. That spark, Paul says, is transformation. And transformation, for him, began the moment he dared to step into the unknown.

Originally from Cameroon, Paul's dream of freedom led him to the United States. While he came to study, something deeper pulled at his spirit—the desire to define life on his own terms. But like many of us, the road to success wasn't linear. It was paved with uncertainty, false starts, and a persistent whisper that said, "There's more."

That whisper grew louder when he joined a network marketing company in the 1990s. Though the financial gains were modest, it exposed him to personal development and lit the first candle: *he could be more—if he chose to grow*. Books, mentors, and mindset work became his tools.

But true transformation came when he and his wife took a leap of faith. With nothing more than a credit card and a dream, they founded a home care business—something they had no prior experience in. What they did have was trust in each other, resilience, and a strong sense of purpose. Over the years, the company grew into a success, not just in numbers, but in impact.

Still, Paul felt something was missing.

That's when Bob Proctor entered the picture. A chance moment during a walk—listening to Bob speak about ignorance being a lack of awareness—became the second spark. Paul realized that he wasn't broken or lacking. He simply didn't *know* yet. And from there, everything changed.

Paul began to understand that success isn't about having all the answers up front. It's about having the *willingness to ask better questions*, to walk into the darkness with faith that the path will light itself. That mindset shift didn't just improve his business—it transformed it. Today, Paul and his wife work fewer hours and generate greater results, because they're operating from alignment, not struggle.

What touched me most was Paul's beautiful metaphor:

"If you light my candle, yours does not go out. It makes the room brighter."

This is the core of his mission now—through his coaching company, Premier Destiny LLC, Paul empowers others to discover the light they've always had inside. His work is rooted in the belief that every individual holds the solution to their own challenges. They just need to *believe* it, *see* it, and *act* on it.

He speaks openly about the excuses that once held him back—his background, his skin color, cultural doubts—and how transformation helped him release those limitations. In doing so, he's become the example he once searched for. And now, his mission is clear: *to light as many candles as he can*.

Paul's story is a reminder that building a business, a legacy, or a movement doesn't start with certainty—it starts with *choice*. A choice to believe. A choice to rise. A choice to walk toward a future that's not yet visible—but always possible.

Whether he's helping seniors through his home care business or entrepreneurs through his coaching, Paul leads from service. His transformation wasn't just personal—it's collective. When he rose, he made it his mission to lift others with him.

If you're waiting for the perfect time, for all the lights to turn green, Paul says this:

27

"It will never all be green. But if you take the first step, the next one will show up."

Let that be the spark.

You can find Paul at premierdestiny.com. And as he reminds us all: *You already have the greatness. Now it's time to light the way.*

Season 12, Episode 29, aired 3/23/2025
recorded 3/22/2025 Washington D.C, US / Lisbon, Portugal

Connect with Paul: https://www.linkedin.com/in/paul-tembunde-2a788b83/
Website: https://www.premieredestiny.com/

4.5 Anmol Singh – The Next Step is Always clear

In this chapter of *The Inspired Choice Chronicles*, we meet Anmol Singh—a trader, investor, entrepreneur, and author whose success story began not with a master plan, but with a simple decision to start.

From his college dorm room, Anmol was just like many of us: unsure of the next step, surrounded by opportunity, yet feeling stuck. His peers were landing internships and jobs. He wasn't. But instead of resigning himself to a path that wasn't his, he asked a powerful question: *What can I do with what I have, right now?*

The answer came in the form of curiosity. With a laptop and a love for technology, he dove into the world of trading—not because he knew where it would lead, but because he wanted to learn. That curiosity turned into passion. Passion turned into skill. And eventually, that skill became a career.

One of the most powerful takeaways from Anmol's story is this: **Action teaches you more than theory ever will.** You can read a hundred books, listen to a thousand podcasts, but if you don't *start*, you don't learn.

"Most people stay stuck in the learning loop," he says. "They're always watching, listening, researching—but never applying. Start now. Let your failures teach you what no textbook can."

Anmol built Live Traders to do just that: empower people to stop waiting and start doing. He doesn't teach gambling or guesswork. He teaches discipline, data, and strategy. His approach to investing mirrors his approach to life: create systems, test results, manage emotion, and stay grounded.

I asked him about trading under pressure. His answer? **It's not about reacting. It's about being ready.** The same way a casino wins over time, traders win when they're consistent and system-driven. And it's the same in life—success doesn't come from one lucky break. It comes from *repetition, resilience, and response*.

We talked about goals, and I expected to hear about five-year visions and multimillion-dollar benchmarks. Instead, Anmol offered something deeper—and simpler:

"The path might be unclear. But the next step? It's always clear. You always know the next thing you need to do."

That next step might be reaching out to someone. Recording your podcast. Making a phone call. Writing the first line of your book. You may not know the whole plan—but you *do* know the next move. And that's all you need.

His analogy of running a marathon stuck with me. At the beginning of the race, out of shape and overwhelmed, he was ready to quit. Until a fellow runner said: *"See that tree over there? Just go to that one."* Tree by tree, step by step, he finished. The finish line didn't come from thinking big—it came from thinking *next*.

When asked about his mentors, Anmol's answer was another inspired choice: *collaboration*. He surrounds himself with experts in areas he's not strong in—health, taxes, accounting—so he can focus on what he does best. This isn't weakness. It's *wisdom*. It's the same principle Napoleon Hill taught: the power of the mastermind.

Anmol lives by what he teaches. He invests in his own coaches, studies what works, and applies relentlessly. That word kept showing up in our conversation: **application**.

"You can read 'Think and Grow Rich' every day," he says. "But if you're not applying what's inside, it's just entertainment. Success is in the action."

This chapter is your reminder that inspired choices don't come from overthinking, doubting, or waiting. They come from action—small steps, repeated often, in the direction of your deepest yes.

So close your eyes for a moment. Ask yourself: *What is the next step I can take today that moves the needle by 1%?* And when the answer comes, don't wait.

Take the step.

You can grab a free copy of Anmol's book at
https://go.anmol.net/
Because knowledge is power—but only if you use it.

And if you're still wondering where to begin, remember this:
You don't need the full path.
You just need to move toward the next tree.

Season 12, Episode 44, aired 30/3/2025

recorded 11/15/24, New York, NY, US / Bavaria, Germany

Connect with Anmol: https://www.livetraders.com/

LinkedIn: https://www.linkedin.com/in/anmolsc/

4.6 Dr. Albert Bramante – No Such Thing as Small Inspiration

In this compelling chapter of *The Inspired Choice Chronicles*, we sit down with Dr. Albert Bramante— psychologist, talent agent, and transformational thought leader. With decades of experience guiding high-performing creatives and entrepreneurs, Albert brings clarity to a truth we often forget: the most powerful shift begins in the mind. From the very start, Albert invites us into a space of growth. A space where failure is not a stop sign, but a signal. A signal to look deeper. To learn. To pivot. To persist. "There's no such thing as failure—only feedback," he reminds us. And that feedback, when used wisely, becomes fuel. Albert's world blends the rigor of psychology with the spontaneity of performance. He works with actors, entrepreneurs, executives, and creators who are under pressure to deliver, perform, and succeed. So, how do the great ones rise? The secret lies in *why* they start—and how often they reconnect to that why. "Every morning and every night, remember your reason. Stay connected to your source. What difference are you here to make?" It's a practice that sounds simple—but it is a practice. One that keeps you grounded in the hard times, and centered in the bright times. We talked about success, and unsurprisingly, Albert doesn't define it by the number of clients, roles, or accolades. For him, success means staying passionate without burning out. It means building a sustainable mindset. One that embraces learning, one that welcomes rejection as redirection, and one that sees every audition, pitch, or presentation as an opportunity to *grow*—not to *prove*.

"You put yourself out there—that's already a win."

So what holds most people back?

Regret. But not the kind you think.

According to Albert—and echoed by psychological research—the greatest source of regret isn't failure. It's the things we *didn't* do. The ideas we didn't pitch. The stages we didn't stand on. The "yes" we didn't say. "The biggest source of regret for most people isn't what they did wrong—it's the opportunities they missed." That line hit me. You, too? What if the cost of not trying is greater than the cost of getting it wrong? To manage the pressure that comes with big goals, Albert teaches a beautiful tool: **The Happy File**. A journal or folder where you collect every piece of positive feedback, meaningful interaction, or success—no matter how small. "When you're in doubt, pull out your happy file. Let it remind you who you are, and why you started." Whether you call it a *Happy File*, *Happiness Chronicles*, or your *Confidence Toolkit*, the point is the same: You've already done remarkable things. Don't let the pressure of the moment make you forget the proof of your path. Albert also shared how he keeps learning. With a PhD, decades of experience, and a thriving client base, you might think he'd have it all figured out. But his mindset says otherwise: "You're never done learning. I still take courses, read books, and work with mentors. The growth mindset never stops." That growth mindset is what leads to his current mission: spreading inspiration on a global scale. Through his book *Rise Above*, his work on stage and behind the scenes, and now multiple books in progress, he's walking the talk. I asked him what final thought he wanted to share with you, dear reader. Here's what he said:

"You never know who you're inspiring. One sentence. One act of kindness. One call to check in—it matters. There's no such thing as a small inspiration. Inspiration is just inspiration."

Let that sink in.

You don't need to be on a stage to be powerful. You don't need a million views to have impact. And you don't need perfect timing to take the next inspired choice.

You just need to act.
To trust.
To show up.

Even if it's just for *one person*—maybe even for yourself.

And if today, that one action is writing your own Happy File, sending that pitch, or following your intuition...

Do it. Because the only thing worse than doing it imperfectly is not doing it at all.

And that, as Albert reminds us, is the true definition of regret.

You can find Dr. Albert Bramante's book *Rise Above* on Amazon and Spotify Audiobooks.
Follow him on Instagram @dralbramante or Facebook at Al Bramante.

And remember:
Keep making those inspired choices.
The world needs your light—especially the one you didn't know you were already shining.

Season 12, Episode 47, aired 4/1/2025
recorded 3/31/2025 New York, NY, US / Lisbon, Portugal

Connect with Albert: https://albertbramante.com/
LinkedIn: https://www.linkedin.com/in/albertbramante/
Book „Rise above the Script": https://amzn.to/42cmaEa

4.7 Jones Loflin – Focused as a Bee

In this energizing chapter of *The Inspired Choice Chronicles*, Caroline sits down with Jones Loflin—keynote speaker, coach, and author of *Juggling Elephants* and *Focused as a Bee*. The conversation buzzes with wisdom, warmth, and a shared love for bees as both a metaphor and a mindset.

From the very first moments, one idea rings clear: busyness does not equal effectiveness.

"The biggest mistake people make when trying to get more done is thinking the answer is to just go faster," Jones shares. "But the real key is stopping—evaluating. Are you prioritizing? Are you clear on what really matters?" Like bees in a hive, we often assume the more motion, the more progress. But it's not motion that counts—it's direction. Jones emphasizes that without clarity, we get caught in the swirl of doing, instead of the flow of being. And being matters—a lot.

"Every bee has one job, and they do it with full focus. That's how they accomplish so much," he explains.

Imagine what your life would look like if you approached each task with that kind of dedication and simplicity. Not chasing twenty priorities. Not overwhelmed by multitasking. Just fully present, fully aligned, fully effective. Caroline, curious about how bees communicate, asks, "Do bees talk to each other?"

The answer? Absolutely—through frequencies, pheromones, even a waggle dance. This is not only fascinating biology—it's a framework for leadership. "In the hive, the queen isn't calling all the shots. Bees communicate laterally. Everyone's tuned in, adjusting to each other in real time," says Jones.

A powerful reminder for leaders: clear direction is crucial, but distributed intelligence—trusting the whole team to observe, respond, and adapt—is where real productivity lives.

Jones Loflin introduces a model from his book *Juggling Elephants* that breaks life into three rings:

1. **Work Ring** – Your professional commitments.
2. **Self Ring** – Your energy, health, and spiritual well-being.
3. **Relationships Ring** – Family, friends, and connections.

"We think we're juggling elephants, but what we really need is a better circus," Jones jokes. His time management tactic? Assess your performance in each ring on a scale of 1–10. Then ask: where am I thriving, and where am I starving? This gentle reflection builds real clarity—and compassionate decision-making. It's not about squeezing in more. It's about choosing better. "You are the ringmaster. You may not be in control of everything, but you *do* influence the outcome."

Change is constant, and Jones breaks it down with wisdom that sticks:

1. **Ask what you need most right now.** Is it clarity, courage, support?
2. **Focus on what you can control.** Let go of the rest.
3. **Talk to someone.** Isolation slows growth. Connection accelerates it.

Caroline reflects on the power of *mastermind*—and how community and reflection help us reframe resistance into action. Together, they explore how reverse engineering from results helps unlock that next inspired step. And that's the key: don't try to figure out the whole journey. "Go as far as you can see," Jones quotes Zig Ziglar, "and when you get there—you can see farther."

Throughout the conversation, one theme hums beneath the surface: We're not here to *do more*—we're here to *be more*.

Jones shares how his own mentors helped him understand his strengths and focus on the *being* behind the doing. He still works with coaches who help him stay aligned in both business and life. His next project? A tool that helps people assess and train their focus—like a muscle. Because being "focused as a bee" isn't a gift. It's a choice. A practice. A skill you can grow.

As always, Caroline brings us back to heart:

"This conversation is like a waggle dance—it gives us direction, energy, and a reason to act."

Jones invites you to explore more at jonesloflin.com/podcast, where you'll find resources for focus, leadership, and intentional living. And if you've been buzzing with ideas during this read—don't let them fly away.

Today's Inspired Choice? Ask yourself:

- What's *my one job* today?
- Which *ring* needs my love and focus?
- What step can I take—as far as I can see?

Then take it. Just like the bees. Just like the ringmaster.

Because when you focus like a bee—you thrive like a hive. And that's the kind of life worth choosing. Every. Single. Day. 🐝

Season 13, Episode 11, aired 4/28/2025
recorded 4/1/2025 Greensboro, NC, US / Lisbon, Portugal

Connect with Jones: http://linkedin.com/in/jonesloflin
Website: http://jonesloflin.com/
Book „Focused as a Bee": https://amzn.to/3R7XE2e
Book "Juggling Elephants": https://amzn.to/3XMFSFt

4.8 Traycee Mayer – The Courage to Lead

Traycee Mayer joined me on this episode of *The Inspired Choice* and shared her incredible journey from corporate leadership to becoming an executive coach, speaker, and author of *The Leadership Contradiction*. With over 40 years of leadership experience, Traycee brings not only practical wisdom but a deeply human message: leadership is no longer about control, it's about connection.

She explained the core idea of her book, which challenges the notion that just because someone holds a leadership title, they're not truly leading. A true leader connects with their people, listens to them, and respects their humanity. If a leader lacks those qualities and acts from ego, fear, or manipulation, they disqualify themselves from the role of leadership—Traycee calls that the leadership contradiction. These kinds of bosses are the ones employees quietly fire by simply walking away from the job.

Traycee made it clear that people today are no longer willing to tolerate poor leadership. In fact, they're reclaiming their lives and demanding more than just a paycheck—they want to be seen, heard, and supported at work. And when they're not, they leave. She talked about how even highly capable people can be pushed out by emotionally disconnected leadership. She's now coaching many senior leaders who are being asked to change their ways because their behavior is driving good talent out the door—and damaging the company.

When we discussed how to create cultures that attract and retain great people, she stressed the importance of human connection. You need to care about the people you lead. That doesn't mean micromanaging—it means listening, checking in, and showing genuine interest in their lives and well-being. She believes that leaders should schedule regular one-on-one meetings, allow the employee to talk most of the time, and keep the meeting focused on connection and support—not status updates.

One of her favorite practices as a leader was the "2 o'clock walk," a daily 10-minute walk around the building with team members. This simple, human moment gave space for real conversation and reconnection. Traycee emphasized that small, consistent efforts like this are what build strong cultures.

She also touched on how modern leadership needs to be individualized. The worst mistake a leader can make, she said, is treating everyone the same. People have different personalities, needs, and work styles. Treating everyone "fairly" in a mechanical way actually causes more harm than good. She told a powerful story about a former manager who reprimanded the entire team for missed sales goals, even though some team members were exceeding their targets. It deflated the entire group. That experience taught her the importance of taking time to help those who are struggling without punishing those who are excelling.

We talked about the outdated concept of work-life balance and how Traycee believes we should just focus on having a life. Work is a part of it, but it shouldn't define us or dominate us. Leaders should support their employees in thriving not just professionally, but personally too.

Traycee also shared her recent trip to Spain where she walked part of the Camino de Santiago. That journey helped her reconnect with her own path and reflect on what's next. One of her upcoming projects is an oracle deck called *The Leader Paths*, inspired by her travels and leadership journey. It's a creative and reflective tool designed to help leaders explore their choices and growth through the metaphor of paths and landscapes. She's pairing it with photography she's taken all over the world and insights drawn from her own leadership evolution.

Today, Traycee runs Be You Leadership and coaches individuals and teams on how to lead from authenticity, emotional intelligence, and clarity. She works with leaders who want to evolve and with teams who are struggling under disconnected leadership. Her passion is helping people see that there is a better way to work and lead—and that they have the power to choose it.

Her final thought was a powerful reminder that even the smallest acts of connection—curiosity, kindness, a few minutes of genuine attention—can change a person's day, and maybe even their life. We don't need to know someone deeply to make a difference. We just have to care enough to ask, listen, and see the human being in front of us.

Traycee is an incredible example of someone who walked away from the system to build something more aligned with her values. If you're struggling under poor leadership or you want to become a better leader yourself, Traycee's message is clear: you always have a choice, and there is help available.

Season 11, Episode 14, aired 1/31/2025
recorded 10/22/2024 Madison, WI, USA / Bavaria, Germany

Connect   with   Traycee:
https://www.linkedin.com/in/trayceemayer/
Website: https://beyouleadership.com/
Book "The Leadership Contradiction": https://amzn.to/4lrpX9N

4.9 Steve Selengut – Retire with Real Returns

Steve Selengut joined me on this episode of *The Inspired Choice* to share the extraordinary story of how he built a 40+ year career as a professional investment manager by focusing on something most people overlook—income. What started in 1970 with a few dividend-paying stocks and a deep respect for multiple income streams became a powerful, proven system that helped Steve manage over $110 million in client portfolios globally.

Steve credits the foundation of his financial mindset to his father, a businessman who had multiple revenue sources coming in from different angles—rental income, insurance, mortgages, a lumberyard, and more. That experience stuck with Steve and guided how he approached investing. From the start, he wasn't chasing flashy growth stocks. He was collecting dividends, studying companies, and building long-term wealth through consistent income.

He left his job in Manhattan when he realized his investment returns were significantly outperforming his salary. That decision led him to launch his own investment management business, where he started coaching others using the exact same strategy he used to grow his own portfolio. Over time, this method evolved into a unique, income-focused investment philosophy that doesn't rely on market timing or risky speculation. When he sold his business in 2023, he had over $110 million under management. That experience became the foundation for his book *Retirement Money Secrets*, and ultimately a new chapter in his career—coaching individuals and advisors on income independence.

One of Steve's core messages is that too many investors obsess over market value, constantly checking how much their portfolio is "worth," without realizing they're just chasing illusions. He says, "Market value fuels the ego. Income fuels the yacht." What really matters is how much your portfolio pays you—month in, month out. Because unless you sell, those unrealized gains don't do you much good. And when markets go down, too many people panic and adjust their life plans instead of seeing it as an opportunity to buy quality assets at a discount.

Steve's approach focuses on generating steady income from diversified, high-quality securities—particularly closed-end funds that are legally required to pay out at least 95% of their earnings. These funds, unlike mutual funds or ETFs, are built to distribute income regularly and often yield 7–10% or more, regardless of market cycles. This income-centric approach means that instead of stressing over price fluctuations, you're focusing on the cash flow your investments generate.

He walked us through four essential principles to reduce investment risk: know the quality of what you invest in, diversify properly, generate income from every asset, and always take your profits. That last one surprised some people—most investors are taught to hold forever. Steve says that's a mistake. If a stock or fund has met your target and given you a good gain, take the profit and either reinvest it or set it aside for when another opportunity shows up.

We talked about how this strategy works even during downturns like the 2008 Great Recession. While many people saw their retirement plans evaporate and had to delay their dreams, Steve's clients continued receiving income and reinvesting at lower prices, ultimately growing their portfolios instead of losing ground.

I asked him how investors can future-proof their portfolios against volatility or rising interest rates, and his answer was simple: you can't. But you can embrace volatility. It's where the opportunities lie. When prices fall, yields rise. And if you've prepared well by holding high-quality, income-generating assets, downturns are nothing to fear.

Steve is now working on launching a new online income investing community filled with tutorials, strategies, and hands-on coaching to help individuals take control of their financial futures. His mission is to educate and empower people to stop relying on Wall Street's models and start building real income that supports real life.

His final thought to listeners was clear and direct: look at your portfolio. Is it generating enough income? If not, you need to rethink your strategy. Whether you do it yourself or with the help of an advisor, demand more income. You deserve it—and the tools are already out there.

You can find Steve's book *Retirement Money Secrets* on Amazon, and visit his website to learn more about coaching and his upcoming programs. Please reach out—he's passionate about helping people take the mystery out of investing and finally feel in control of their money.

Season 12, Episode 57, aired 4/6/2025
recorded 12/5/24 John's Island, SC, US / Bavaria, Germany

Connect with Steve:
https://www.linkedin.com/in/privateinvestmentmanagement/

Book "RETIREMENT MONEY SECRETS":
https://amzn.to/3FXkWp6

Join RMS Income Investing Community here:
https://www.skool.com/rms-income-investing-community-2827/about?ref=aea4d531723f40989f5d4a948d4e2857

4.10 Cristine Hull – The Future of Healing

When I sat down with Cristine Hull for our interview on *The Inspired Choice* podcast, I knew I was about to meet someone extraordinary. What followed wasn't just an inspiring conversation—it was a powerful transmission of energy, insight, and transformation. Cristine Hull isn't your typical mental health expert. She's a visionary—a fusion of ancient wisdom and quantum science. With a doctorate in Natural Medicine and a master's in Psychology, she's the creator of *Quantum Wholeness Meditation* and author of *10 Ways to Balance Your Brain Chemistry*. Her mission: help people move beyond survival into full-spectrum healing. What struck me most wasn't just her brilliance—it was her story. Cristine's path began with a deeply personal moment. She shared how her grandfather, a spiritual man and engineer, asked for a book on quantum physics on his deathbed. In his final lucid moments, bridging worlds, he sought knowledge—not just science, but the truth beneath it. Years later, when Cristine sought her next step in education, she felt his presence guiding her to Quantum University. Despite already holding a psychology degree, she knew her PhD belonged there. That decision changed her life—and ultimately, the lives of thousands. From this union of science and soul, *Quantum Wholeness Meditation* was born. Unlike traditional methods like Transcendental Meditation, Cristine's approach is efficient and intuitive. In just nine minutes, practitioners can experience shifts that might otherwise take 40 minutes a day. Her work connects people around the globe—from South Africa to Alaska—in virtual group meditations, forming what she calls "conscious collectives"—communities of lightworkers raising the planet's frequency.

But that's just one facet of her work.

Cristine also leads in the field of integrative mental health. She introduced me to the "Four Bodies, Four Medicines" framework—a holistic approach to healing. We don't just have a physical body, she explained. We also have a vital body (responsive to energy medicine), a mental body (shaped by thoughts), and a quantum body—the deepest level of self. It was this model that helped a CEO client, teetering on burnout, return to balance. Cristine used a "quantum formula" to recalibrate her adrenal system—not a drug, but what she calls "information medicine." Within 60 days, the client's sleep improved, her energy stabilized, and her sense of self returned. This is the future of mental health: frequency over pharmaceuticals, intention over prescriptions, community over isolation. Cristine's mission is to create that future. But the path hasn't been easy. She opened up about the challenges of blending natural medicine with clinical psychology. At one point, she sold supplements in her practice—only to learn later this conflicted with professional guidelines. Her intentions were pure, and her clients benefited, but the system wasn't ready for her vision. Instead of stopping, she evolved. Cristine founded *LoveSolve Academy*, a school—not a clinic—where clients become students and healing becomes empowerment. Within this sacred space, people don't just heal—they learn to become healers. They take these tools into their families, businesses, and communities. Because Cristine isn't just offering healing. She's creating healers. That mission fuels her most ambitious project yet: *One Million Meditators*. When she asked the universe for a number to guide her next step, the message was clear—one million meditators. And so the movement was born. Through AMillionAtOne.com, Cristine is building a global network of heart-centered people committed to elevating consciousness through daily practice. The number is symbolic—but the impact is very real. She reminded me: healing isn't linear. It's layered. And when we approach it with love, intention, and the wisdom of the quantum field, we don't just heal ourselves—we heal generations forward and back.

Toward the end of our interview, we talked about goals—and of course, Cristine has many. She's currently focused on reaching her first 1,000 meditators, expanding research on her methods, publishing in academic journals, and scaling her certification programs to train others in her work. But her final message wasn't about goals. It was about alignment. Cristine encourages us to raise our frequency—to live in the vibration of joy, wholeness, and fulfilment across all five areas of life: physical, emotional, mental, spiritual, and relational. When we align all five, she believes, we become unstoppable. To sit with Cristine Hull is to sit with a soul on fire. Her science is solid, her vision is expansive, and her heart is wide open. If you've ever questioned whether healing could be both spiritual and scientific, practical and profound—Cristine is your proof. She's not just making inspired choices. She's inviting the world to do the same. Visit Cristine at www.cristinehull.com (no "h" in Cristine!), join the meditation movement at https://amillionatone.com/home, and remember:

Your frequency is your future.

Season 13, Episode 25, aired 5/5/2025
recorded 4/10/25 Hyrum, UT, US / Lisbon, Portugal
Connect with Cristine: www.cristinehull.com

4.11 Shelley Devine – The Art of Healing

What if healing didn't come in the form of a prescription—but in brushstrokes, colors, and quiet moments of soul-led creation? Shelley Devine knows this deeply. As an evidential medium, spiritual coach, and creator of *Awaken Your Creative Spirit*, Shelley doesn't just talk about transformation—she invites people to experience it, one canvas at a time.

When I sat down with Shelley for *The Inspired Choice*, I was immediately struck by her warmth, presence, and joyful energy. Her journey into mediumship and intuitive creativity is not just a story of discovering spiritual gifts—it's a lesson in how healing and wholeness often emerge from unexpected places. Shelley's own awakening came in 2020. What she had long written off as imagination—voices, visions, feelings—turned out to be her intuitive connection to Spirit. "I always thought I was just a very imaginative girl," she told me. "Turns out they were spirits trying to communicate." That realization changed everything. Shelley embraced her gifts as a psychic and medium, and began integrating them into her lifelong passion for art. The result? A revolutionary method of intuitive painting that doesn't require technical skill—only a willingness to listen inwardly. "It's not about being a great artist," Shelley said. "You don't even need to know how to hold a paintbrush. You just need to be open." In her workshops and courses, students are encouraged to let go of perfectionism, drop into presence, and let Spirit guide the brush. What emerges is more than art. It's healing. It's self-reclamation. Her *Awaken Your Creative Spirit* program is an eight-week experience rooted in mindfulness, meditation, self-expression, and spiritual connection. Shelley walks her students through guided painting sessions that unfold like a dance between intuition and inspiration. "It's a sacred practice," she said, "not just painting—but learning to receive, to be present, and to let go." The experience is both personal and powerful. One moment you're choosing a color based on how it calls to you; the next, you're recognizing an image or symbol on the canvas that holds deep meaning. "A bluebird, a whale, a shape—you don't go in with a plan," Shelley explained. "You ask Spirit, 'What would you like to show me today?'" Her approach is more than creative expression—it's intuitive activation. Through letting go of expectations and embracing imperfection, her students access clarity, healing, and often, profound personal breakthroughs. "You're the artist of your life," Shelley told me. "You're the creator. So create it." But her work doesn't stop at the canvas. Shelley is also passionate about making space for neurodivergent creatives—those whose brains and energies don't follow the traditional mold. "Creative minds work differently," she said. "We may be working on six projects at once. That's not a flaw—it's just how we're wired." She proudly contributed a chapter to the bestselling book *Beyond the Ordinary*, highlighting how creativity and neurodivergence intersect to create new paths for expression and healing. This isn't just a concept for Shelley. It's her lived experience. Growing up in an abusive household, art was her refuge. "I would hide in the closet and draw unicorns," she shared. "Even back then, art saved me." Decades later, when she lost three loved ones in just a few weeks—including her soulmate best friend—it was art that carried her through the grief. "She told me before she passed, 'Don't let this break you. Keep painting.'" At first, it was hard. Shelley described dragging herself to her art room, not even sure she could lift a brush. But when she did, the tears flowed. One painting—*The Deep Sorrow*—captured that raw moment of loss. It became a fan favorite, not because it was beautiful in a traditional sense, but because it was honest. "I never paint anything negative," she said, "but that one needed to come out. And once it did, I felt relief. I remembered who I was." That's what Shelley offers her students, clients, and community: a return to self. Whether through mediumship, coaching, or her creative courses, her work is about reminding people of their wholeness. "Art is healing," she said. "It's the soul reaching out to say, 'Here I am.'"

I asked Shelley about the difference between psychic work, mediumship, and channeling—terms that often get confused. Her answer was clear and grounded. "Psychic work is about the here and now—what's happening with the person in front of you," she said. "Mediumship is connecting with loved ones who've passed on. And channeling? That's when you connect with guides or higher beings to bring through wisdom or messages." In all of it, Shelley emphasized the importance of trust. "You don't need to understand everything right away," she said. "But if you're curious, if you feel pulled, get a reading. It can be life-changing." Her biggest advice for skeptics or first-timers? "Just try. You'll know when it's real. There's no way I could know some of the things that come through. When someone hears a name, a gesture, or a detail that's so personal—it opens them. It heals something." Today, Shelley continues to lead, teach, and create. Her next project? A course based on her book *Artful Affirmations*, which guides people through themed mixed-media paintings infused with symbolic meaning and powerful affirmations. It's a full-circle integration of art, spirit, and healing—Shelley Devine's soul work in action.

If you want to connect with Shelley, you can visit her at infinitesoulreadings.com or reach out via email at infinitesoulreadings@gmail.com. Whether you're seeking intuitive guidance, creative expansion, or simply a reminder that you're not alone—Shelley is a gentle, powerful guide.

Her parting words were simple and unforgettable:

"We are infinite souls. And when we remember that, we become unstoppable."

Season 12, Episode 65, aired 4/10/2025

recorded 4/9/2025 XY, US / Lisbon, Portugal
Connect with Shelley: https://infinitesoulreadings.com/

4.12 Sue Bortone – Pivot with Purpose

Sue Bortone never intended to become a recruitment powerhouse. She began her career as a creative in a top New York ad agency, dreaming of campaigns and storyboards rather than candidate pipelines. Yet after two years of loving the brand work she was doing, she found herself craving variety, a broader canvas of experiences. When she walked into a recruitment firm to find herself a new position, she didn't just land a job—she discovered her natural superpower: connecting people. That impulsive choice at age twenty-five launched her into a world where her knack for conversation, her ability to listen and match ambitions with opportunities, would become the foundation of Noble Talent Group. By the time the pandemic swept across the globe, Sue had already helped build recruitment offices from Boston to San Francisco. She had driven sales teams, placed hundreds of candidates, and earned her badge as a Forbes Council contributor. But when COVID forced mass layoffs—even in her own company—she faced the same crossroads many entrepreneurs do: pivot or perish. Sue chose pivot. She went back to school to become certified in change management at Harvard, recognizing that organizations needed far more than headcount to evolve; they needed strategic culture shifts, new processes, real guidance on how to grow in turbulent times. Armed with fresh insights, Sue returned to the recruiting trenches and spotted a structural flaw: every major firm she observed was charging sky-high, opaque fees—up to 100 percent mark-ups—that squeezed both clients and the talent they depended on. Rather than accept this status quo, she launched Noble Talent Group with a transparent model: fifteen percent for permanent hires, twenty-five percent for project-based work. The result was immediate. Startups and midsize agencies, the ones hungry to scale but cautious with cash, flocked to her. They saved money, they retained more of their own revenue for growth, and they put more into the pockets of the freelancers and new hires who were building their businesses. Sue often reminds me, "When you remove hidden fees, clients see you as a partner rather than a vendor," and the network ripple-effect took hold.

Sue's approach doesn't stop at fees. Every candidate search is framed by a change-management lens. She asks why a role exists, not just what it is. She digs into team communication, the invisible influencers, and the onboarding roadmaps that make or break new hires, especially in remote cultures. Too many companies believe one extra headcount solves broken processes; Sue knows it's the right processes that guide headcounts to success. When Noble steps in, they deliver not only talent but also an advisory blueprint—detailed handoff points, weekly check-ins, milestone metrics—so the new marketing manager or creative director isn't left to sink or swim. The pandemic also accelerated an existing trend Sue had watched closely: the shift toward freelance and contract work in marketing. Even roles that once demanded full-time commitment—demand generation, lifecycle management, performance marketing—have migrated to project-based engagements. Data-driven functions, in particular, thrive under short-term sprints because results are quantifiable and the ROI is immediate. Sue's advice for agency founders and CMOs is simple: modularize your offerings. Package email automation or social media strategy into four-week pilots, and let top talent rotate through your projects. You'll not only stay agile, you'll attract professionals who value variety and autonomy. None of this success would surprise Sue's mentees at She Runs It, where she serves on the board and sponsors roundtables for women in media and advertising. Her perspective on mentorship extends beyond one-on-one calls: it lives in small peer groups, accountability circles, and virtual coffee chats. She's witnessed the magic that happens when five professionals gather with a single question, exchange insights, and leave with concrete action steps. Sue has learned that the richest mentorship often emerges not from a guru-and-student dynamic but from a community where every voice contributes. That's why she champions both formal advisory services and informal mastermind gatherings. Sue's personal toolkit is just as pragmatic. She sets goals at every scale—whether it's reaching out to ten new contacts this week, migrating her firm to a new software platform by Friday, or finally publishing her first by-line as a Forbes contributor. She keeps those goals visible on whiteboards, habit-tracking apps, even sticky notes on her bathroom mirror. That discipline came from years on sales teams, where daily quotas and performance dashboards were non-negotiable. Today, as a founder leading a remote enterprise, it's the micro-milestones that keep her momentum alive when laundry piles up or technical glitches threaten to derail her focus. At the end of every conversation with me, Sue returns to the same core principle: obstacles are not roadblocks but the very mountains you're meant to climb. When you hit budget cuts, team turnover, or stalled growth, the instinct is to look for detours, workarounds, or exit ramps. Sue's counsel is to go through the mountain. Push straight toward it, break it down one rock at a time, and you'll emerge on the other side stronger, wiser, and more prepared for the next ascent.

If you take anything from Sue Bortone's journey, let it be this: align your career with your inherent talents, strip away barriers between you and your clients—be they hidden fees or dysfunctional processes—and build a community that fuels mutual growth. Package your services for today's talent market, set goals that force daily progress, and never underestimate the power of pushing straight through your biggest challenges. That's how you transform from an accidental recruiter into a CEO Oracle, and how you guide countless entrepreneurs across the peaks of their own mountains—one inspired choice at a time.

Season 12, Episode 79, aired 4/17/2025
recorded 4/8/25 New York, NY, US / Lisbon, Portugal

Connect with Sue: https://www.nobletalent.group/

4.13 Kristen Chimack – The Cost of Staying

When Kristen Chimack first told herself to pay attention to the whispers, she could never have predicted how loud they'd grow—and how profoundly they'd reshape her life. As a Fortune 50 executive, she'd climbed every rung of the corporate ladder, mastered every presentation and budget cycle, and earned the prestige she'd worked toward since college. But with each passing year, she found herself waking up to the same gnawing question: "Is this really who I am?" The subtle discomfort in her chest grew into a daily ache, and by her late thirties those whispers were impossible to ignore. She began tallying moments of dread on her commute, feeling as though she'd become the person the company wanted, rather than herself. Kristen's decision to step away wasn't sparked by a single, dramatic moment, but by dozens of small signals—missed family dinners, a bored mind in strategy meetings, a hollow satisfaction at promotions. She likens these to body alerts that say, 'something's off,' and once she started listening, the path forward became clear. Closer to fifty, the whispers turned into an unmistakable pull toward authenticity. She began researching how to channel her experience into coaching, took courses in life design and change management, and—just as importantly—allowed herself to grieve what she was losing. There was grief for the title she'd fought so hard to keep, grief for colleagues who'd become distant when she left, and grief for the predictable paycheck she knew she'd miss. It was during a casual lunch of chips and queso with her eleven-year-old niece that Kristen realized how far she'd come. Between bites, her niece asked, "Aunt Kristen, do you regret leaving your job?" The simplicity and sincerity of that question struck Kristen harder than any boardroom critique ever could. She found herself explaining to a child that regret was not part of her vocabulary. Instead, she shared how leaving had given her the freedom to define success on her own terms: not by corner offices and stock options, but by the luxury of time with loved ones, the excitement of building something new, and the daily choice to wake up excited rather than exhausted. That conversation, winding through the reasons for and against staying, became the seed for her first book, *The Cost of Staying*, where she explores the silent price we pay when we ignore our deepest urges. In *The Cost of Staying*, Kristen walks readers through her own "growth through grief spiral," a process of noticing the whispers, leaning into discomfort, letting go of old identities, and daring to imagine new possibilities. She dissects pivotal moments—staying too long in a relationship, clinging to a job that no longer fit, walking away from friendships that had outlived their purpose—and shows how each act of release opened space for authenticity. Her narrative is honest about the unexpected grief that follows big changes: the fading of long-term friendships, the awkward silences at reunions, the sting of watching people move on without you. But she also offers a roadmap out of that heavy place: curiosity, compassion, community, and the courage to rewrite your own story. Kristen's coaching philosophy reflects that same journey. She starts every session by asking clients to remember what they loved doing at ages five, twelve, and eighteen. Those childhood passions, she argues, hold clues to our truest selves—long before budgets and career ladders warped our sense of purpose. She pairs that exercise with a deep dive into core values: transparency, creativity, service. When a client realizes their current role violates those values—say, marketing in a way that feels inauthentic or managing people without genuine connection—they don't simply change jobs. Instead, they learn to craft a path that honors both their professional goals and their inner compass. One of her most memorable success stories involved a mid-level manager trapped in organizational politics. By identifying her client's core values of authenticity and meaningful relationships, Kristen helped her reframe internal meetings as opportunities to build trust rather than political maneuvering. Two promotions later, that same client now leads a division with enthusiastic buy-in from teammates who know exactly why she's there and what she stands for. Kristen's role was never about network matches or resume tweaks—it was about restoring alignment between an individual's deepest motivations and their day-to-day reality.

Kristen's methods extend beyond one-on-one coaching into small peer circles and retreats. She believes some of the most potent insights come from the spontaneous questions of others—often children—or from watching a group wrestle with a single challenge. Later this year she will blend her coaching business with her event-planning expertise to host retreats where women can connect over guided reflections, heartfelt conversations, and the shared acknowledgment that no one climbs these mountains alone. Imagine three days of morning workshops on shedding outdated beliefs, midday hikes to symbolize the ascent past old pain points, and evening bonfires where newfound clarity sparks real-world commitments. That's the kind of immersive, transformational experience Kristen is eager to create. Through it all, Kristen defines success not by revenue streams or bestseller lists—though her column and her book launch have been celebrated milestones—but by the quality of her daily life. She measures it in the laughter over family dinners, the satisfaction of launching a new program, and yes, the occasional chips and queso lunch where profound questions can come from the most unexpected sources. She sets goals with the same precision she once reserved for corporate projects: a certain number of coaching sessions per month, a draft of her next article by week's end, the first retreat. These micro-goals keep her momentum alive without sacrificing her newfound flexibility. As the interview winds down, Kristen offers her signature advice: notice the whispers, honor them, and recognize that you're never too old to change. She reminds us that every pivotal point in life carries both loss and opportunity—that grief is the currency we pay for growth, and letting go is the key that unlocks our truest potential. If you take nothing else from her story, let it be this: the mountain in front of you can become the view behind you, and the only regret worth fearing is the one planted by inaction. feels, finally, like your own.

Season 13, Episode 9, aired 4/27/2025
recorded 4/14/25 Illinois Area, US / Lisbon, Portugal
Connect with Kristen: https://kristenchimack.com/

4.14 Birgitta Visser – Alchemy of Soul Transformation

Birgitta Visser's path into soul empowerment began with the reality of surviving what so many would rather forget. Early experiences of abuse and loss left invisible scars that no outward success could heal. A thriving modeling career offered validation, yet underneath, the unspoken weight of trauma persisted. Grief for her father's death at fourteen mingled with the shame of secrets she carried into adulthood, and even as her professional life flourished, Birgitta felt a persistent emptiness that no accolade could fill.

In her thirties, she recognized that healing would require confronting each wound rather than hiding it. An unexpected invitation from a counselor led her first into Reiki, where she learned that energetic blockages could be gently released through focused intention. Over eighteen months of disciplined study she discovered the transformative power of channeling divine guidance and light language, tools that allowed her to translate inner messages into healing frequencies. Each new modality—from emotional freedom tapping to angelic reiki to holistic nutrition—became another thread in the tapestry of her recovery.

Birgitta learned that past lives and ancestral patterns often echo through present challenges. A profound Akashic-record session dissolved the karmic ties that had kept a former partner tethered to her pain, freeing both of them from a cycle of repetition. In that release she saw how shifting frequency could literally change reality. She began to teach what she had practiced: guiding others to alchemize their suffering into wisdom, to stop judging experience as good or bad, and simply to honor it as a necessary step on the journey toward wholeness.

Her coaching philosophy rests on the conviction that everyone possesses an inner authority—a soul voice drowned out by societal expectations and egoic fear. By learning to ask powerful questions and then trusting the subtle answers that arise, her clients reconnect with the deepest parts of themselves. Birgitta teaches that thoughts are energetic seeds cast into the universal field; by consciously choosing empowering beliefs, individuals can reshape both internal landscapes and external circumstances. She encourages each person to claim responsibility for their life, to step out of the molds imposed by family, culture, or career, and to rediscover what truly makes their heart sing.

Over the past year, Birgitta has channeled those core principles into three bestselling books and is preparing a fourth on plant medicine, born from her own experiences with ancient South American ceremonies. She envisions retreats where participants will journey through guided meditations, ceremonial plant work, and light-language activations—immersive rites of passage designed to accelerate transformation. These gatherings will unite her two worlds: the spiritual practices that first rescued her and the event-design skills she honed in her pre-coaching career.

Underpinning every program and publication is Birgitta's unwavering belief in co-creation. She insists that no one heals in isolation; every interaction is an opportunity for mutual illumination. Workshops she leads often include peer exchanges, where spontaneous questions from fellow seekers yield insights more potent than any lecture. Her role is not to dispense answers, but to hold space for each person's unique wisdom to emerge.

Birgitta measures success not by financial metrics or social media followings, but by the subtle shifts she witnesses in people's daily lives: the lightness in their steps, the courage to speak their truth, the capacity to see challenge as a teacher rather than an enemy. She reminds all who cross her path that every experience—no matter how painful—is simply that: an experience. Judgment only binds us to a limited perspective;

when we release our resistance, we open to a reality defined by possibility.

In the end, Birgitta's message is both radical and simple: life can be better, but it first demands radical honesty and the willingness to feel our discomfort fully. We are, each of us, divine alchemists capable of transforming leaden sorrow into golden purpose. By shifting our consciousness, embracing our wholeness, and returning to love as our guiding principle, we step into the highest expression of who we really are. And in doing so, we not only heal ourselves but light the way for others to follow.

Season 10, Episode 66, aired 1/13/2025
recorded 10/11/24 Spain / Bavaria, Germany

Connect with Birgitta: https://www.powersoulhealing.com/
Book „Be-com-ing authentically": https://amzn.to/4jqBNj1
Book „Child oft he Sun": https://amzn.to/3Glhsgi

4.15 Marsha Familaro Enright – Great books, Greater Minds

Marsha Familaro Enright's vision for education emerged from a lifetime spent both inside and outside traditional schools. After founding a Montessori program in 1990 that served children up to age fifteen, she watched with growing concern as colleges abandoned the rich content and rigorous methods that once formed free, independent thinkers. Convinced that graduates were ill prepared to participate fully in a free society, she set out to build an institution grounded in classical liberal principles and Montessori-inspired practices. That institution, Reliance College, opens its doors in 2026—but long before then, Marsha has been testing and refining her approach through a program she calls the Great Connections Seminar.

Since 2009, students from age sixteen to twenty-four have gathered each summer for a week of immersive study, guided not by lectures but by carefully selected readings from the so-called Great Books. Physics passages sit alongside poetry, history lines up with economic treatises, and each selection is chosen because its ideas still shape our world—even if most people today remain unaware of that influence. Rather than delivering authoritative interpretations, Marsha's instructors create an environment in which students learn to read deeply, discern an author's argument, and draw their own conclusions about how these timeless works apply to modern life.

By the end of the week, more than three-quarters of participants report a profound shift in confidence and self-reliance. They discover how to judge for themselves whether an idea is true or useful, to test its impact on personal behavior, and to distinguish between passing fads and enduring wisdom. Friendships form quickly as young thinkers bond over spirited debates, and many of those connections endure well into adulthood. Experiential learning outings—whether tracing the steps of ancient philosophers on a trip to Greece or walking the cobblestones of revolutionary Paris—reinforce the link between abstract texts and the real world. Each overseas journey combines local history, integrated cultural context, and shared meals to deepen both knowledge and camaraderie.

Marsha's next milestone comes when Reliance College launches its full liberal arts curriculum. Admission will require an abridged version of the Great Connections Seminar, ensuring that every new student arrives ready to engage, question, and create. In the college's classrooms, the four pillars of environment—physical, psychological, social, and academic—are each designed to foster intrinsic motivation. Lecture halls give way to collaborative studios, formal desks yield to flexible work tables, and walls bristle with student-created mind maps instead of rote rules. Just as Montessori classrooms ignite children's natural curiosity, this model aims to sustain it through the young adult years, producing graduates whose discipline emerges from genuine interest rather than external compulsion.

Marsha sees one of the biggest misconceptions in education as the belief that knowledge must be poured into passive students, rather than discovered and owned by active learners. To combat that, every lesson at Reliance is structured so that no one can hide behind an assumed answer. Faculty members guide students toward questions rather than delivering facts, and assessment focuses on the ability to synthesize across domains—connecting a concept in political philosophy to a problem in environmental science, for instance—rather than memorizing isolated details.

Parents who worry about their children's schooling are invited to reclaim agency by choosing environments aligned with their family values. Whether that means investigating a Montessori-inspired preschool or applying to a seminar that guarantees genuine engagement, families are encouraged to remain vigilant, to visit classrooms in session, and to demand that educational settings both challenge and inspire. Education, in Marsha's view, is not a one-size-fits-all service but a partnership in which students, teachers, and families share responsibility for purpose and progress.

Behind the college's ambitious plans stands Marsha's personal network of mentors and influences. Her husband has served as her closest advisor, offering steadfast support and creative insights. From Maria Montessori she learned the power of self-directed learning, and from thinkers like Ayn Rand she embraced the idea that clarity of thought and personal productivity form the bedrock of a flourishing life. Those inspirations feed into both her writing—most recently a series of papers on the philosophy of biology—and her ongoing research into how life itself can be understood as an integrated, self-ordering process.

As Volume 3 of this series unveils, Marsha Familaro Enright's work exemplifies the principle of being "Built to Give." Every curriculum element, every seminar activity, and every campus design decision springs from a desire to give learners the tools they need to think freely, act boldly, and contribute meaningfully to the world around them. Her story reminds us that education is not a commodity to be consumed, but a gift to be shared—and that by empowering each individual to become self-reliant, we ultimately strengthen our collective capacity for growth and innovation. In this new era of classical liberal learning, every reader is invited to become not merely a consumer of ideas, but a deliberate architect of their own intellectual and moral freedom.

Season 12, Episode 77, aired 4/16/2025
recorded 4/15/25 Chicago, IL, US / Lisbon, Portugal

Connect with Marsha: http://www.reliancecollege.org/

4.16 Charley Johnson – The Consciousness C-Suite

Charley Johnson's conviction that consciousness must become as integral to business as finance or marketing grew from watching firsthand how wellness initiatives, despite good intentions, failed to heal the divisions that persist within organizations. After decades navigating the corporate world, leading a charitable foundation, and studying under an enlightened teacher, he realized that mindfulness and yoga, while valuable, address symptoms rather than root causes. What companies really need is someone whose sole mandate is to bring clarity, cohesion, and expanded awareness to the decision-making table. Thus the role of Chief Consciousness Officer emerged—a tactical position designed not to replace wellness programs but to amplify their impact by focusing on the underlying source of all human interaction.

Rather than prescribing another employee perk, this new executive role operates at the intersection of spiritual insight and business acumen. By treating consciousness as the wellspring from which all ideas, strategies, and relationships flow, the CCO helps leaders move beyond the dualistic thinking that keeps organizations stuck. Where traditional consultants diagnose problems and prescribe solutions, the Chief Consciousness Officer guides executives to recognize the mind's tendency to polarize—Republican versus Democrat, profit versus purpose, us versus them—and then to transcend those limiting frameworks by anchoring every initiative in a deeper sense of unity and purpose.

One nonprofit board that had struggled for half a decade discovered the power of this approach in just a few weeks. Longstanding debates over strategy, stalled by entrenched biases and personality conflicts, suddenly gave way to swift, unanimous decisions when Charley entered their meetings as a neutral facilitator. Unencumbered by alliances or past disputes, he listened impartially to every perspective, wove together common themes, and reframed proposals in a way that addressed mutual needs. By removing the ownership of ideas from any single individual, he transformed the group's dynamic: what once dragged on for years was resolved in days, proving that when consciousness is elevated, so too is organizational performance.

At the heart of this work lies an understanding that the mind—our habitual, dualistic tool—can only take us so far. It interprets reality through the lens of past conditioning, inevitably creating conflict when two intelligent people arrive at opposing conclusions. Consciousness, in contrast, is the unifying field from which the mind draws its raw material. By teaching executives to recognize their thoughts as provisional rather than absolute, and by cultivating the ability to tap directly into that source, the Chief Consciousness Officer unlocks a reservoir of creativity, resilience, and collaborative potential that no amount of training or process redesign can achieve alone.

This shift also dissolves the false binary between profit and purpose. Companies no longer need to choose one at the expense of the other, because true sustainability arises when both objectives are held in tandem. Purpose-driven initiatives fuel employee engagement, brand loyalty, and long-term vision, while healthy profits provide the resources to scale meaningful impact. When consciousness is woven into corporate DNA, these aims reinforce rather than counteract each other, generating a virtuous cycle of growth that benefits all stakeholders—from investors to the communities they serve.

Charley's own journey prepared him uniquely for this pioneering role. Years spent studying diverse spiritual traditions, from the disciplined practices of his teacher to the philosophic maps of scholars like David R. Hawkins, taught him to shed personal bias and to appreciate the universal truths beneath disparate belief systems. This deep comparative study forged in him a rare neutrality: the ability to see every cultural, ideological, or functional perspective as a valid expression of the same underlying reality. It is this stance—rooted in expansive awareness rather than tribal loyalty—that empowers him to guide organizations through the unprecedented shifts they now face.

Looking ahead, Charley's immediate goal is to secure the first corporate appointment of a Chief Consciousness Officer, demonstrating its transformative power on a large scale. With that success, he intends to serve as a catalyst for other companies, advising them on how to integrate consciousness into their leadership structures and, eventually, to identify and train their own CCOs. Already, interest in the role has spread rapidly through podcasts, LinkedIn conversations, and word-of-mouth, signaling that the appetite for this level of insight is growing as fast as the challenges it addresses.

At its core, instituting a Chief Consciousness Officer is an act of giving: a commitment to invest in the invisible forces that shape decisions, relationships, and culture. By placing responsibility for collective awareness into the hands of a dedicated leader, organizations send a powerful message that human potential matters as much as quarterly returns. In this way, the role becomes not just a new title on the org chart, but a beacon for a more integrated, compassionate, and effective way of doing business—one that truly lives up to the promise of being "Built to Give."

Season 12, Episode 81, aired 4/18/2025
recorded 4/17/25 Salt Lake City, UT, US / Lisbon, Portugal

Connect with Charley:
https://www.linkedin.com/in/cjconsciousness/

4.17 Tracey Sundkvist – Think big, achieve more

Tracey Sundkvist built her reputation on guiding entrepreneurs through the discomfort that accompanies real growth. She often reminds clients that change always comes with pain—either the slow burn of staying stuck or the sharp sting of transformation—and urges them to choose the pain that serves them best. This lesson underpins every principle she teaches, drawing on a deep foundation of psychology, systems theory, and the latest in neuroscience.

Her signature mindset shift begins with goal-setting: too many business owners aim for what feels safe and reasonable, never discovering the heights they're capable of reaching. Tracey challenges them to think audaciously, to dare massive, seemingly impossible targets. By stretching beyond familiar limits, entrepreneurs uncover strengths they would otherwise never tap into—and the victories they do achieve, however small, blaze a trail toward ever greater possibilities.

Neuroscience offers the second pillar of Tracey's approach. It explains why old habits feel unshakable—neurons that fire together really do wire together, carving deep ruts in the brain. Yet the same research shows that our minds remain remarkably plastic throughout life. The path forward is simple in theory but demanding in practice: we must deliberately forge new neural pathways by practicing fresh ways of thinking, speaking, and acting until they become our new default. In coaching sessions, Tracey designs exercises that break old patterns and reinforce new ones, helping clients stay focused long enough to wire a different future.

Time and again, she sees this method reshape personal brands from the inside out, especially in care-focused fields like healthcare services. Practitioners who entered their businesses to help others find themselves undercharging out of empathy, only to quietly resent the financial strain. Once they confront the internal beliefs that equate compassion with self-sacrifice, they begin to price their expertise fairly, liberating both themselves and their patients. The result isn't greed—it's the ability to give at a higher level, sustaining growth that benefits everyone.

Scaling beyond that first breakthrough requires yet another shift: admitting that no one can—and should—go it alone. Entrepreneurs who build the first six-figure revenue often feel invincible, only to be tripped up by complexity when they aim higher. Tracey advises assembling a "board of smarter people": mentors, advisors, peer groups who bring fresh perspectives and specialized know-how. With that collaborative support, leaders avoid blind spots and accelerate progress without bearing every weight themselves.

Tracey credits her own transformation to the coach who taught her the neuroscience-based methods she now shares. That mentor didn't simply fill her head with information, but asked questions so penetrating they forced her to wrestle with hidden fears and assumptions. Those long, reflective pauses—the questions that have no easy answers—became the crucible in which Tracey forged her most powerful insights, and they're the tools she passes on to her clients today.

Looking ahead, she's channeling this framework into a new initiative: strengthening chiropractic practices as pillars of preventive healthcare. By helping chiropractors build thriving, resilient businesses, she intends to expand access to care that keeps people healthy before they become sick—another example of choosing the pain of innovation over the pain of decline. In Tracey's world, every entrepreneur who masters these shifts becomes not just a stronger business owner, but a giver of higher-impact services to their community.

Her closing reminder is both sobering and liberating: the pain of change is inevitable, but it need not be debilitating. By leaning into purposeful discomfort—turning old wounds into launch pads for new strengths—any leader can choose the better pain, and in doing so, unlock a capacity to give that reaches far beyond the bottom line. In the end, that choice is the hallmark of every inspired entrepreneur.

Season 13, Episode 5, aired 4/24/2025
recorded 4/23/25 Port Elizabeth, South Africa / Lisbon, Portugal

Website: https://www.mutantdynamix.com/
Connect with Tracey:
https://go.oncehub.com/ExplorewithTracey

4.18 Allison Williams – Alignment over Prestige

Allison K. Williams discovered early that true transformation begins with a deceptively simple question: is the change you seek something you're running toward, or something you're running away from? This question wasn't plucked from a textbook—it was born of her own reckoning after two departures from high-paying corporate roles. The first came unbidden, when a company she had poured herself into laid her off without warning. The shock of suddenly losing both title and income forced her into a period of soul-searching she had never anticipated. With the cushion of a generous severance, Allison chose not to cling to the perceived safety of her next six-figure offer, but to step back and ask herself what she truly wanted.

That decision led her to partner in a startup executive-search firm—a venture with no guarantees, no salary, no benefits. Yet within nine years they built a thriving business, proving that betting on one's own vision can yield richer rewards than any corporate ladder. Still, as the first whisper of misalignment crept in again, Allison realized that success measured by revenue alone would never satisfy the deeper urge to serve. She and her partner amicably ended their collaboration, and she once more struck out on her own, this time as an executive coach devoted to helping others break free from the very patterns that had once entrapped her.

What she teaches her clients is drawn directly from her own journey. The first step is always to pause—and to imagine, however reluctantly, what an ideal day would look like if nothing stood in the way. Most high achievers flinch at such exercises, believing it selfish to dream while responsibilities loom large. Yet Allison insists that clarity about one's aspirations—whether it's more sleep, a guilt-free vacation, or simply time with family—lays the groundwork for sustainable change. By reversing from that vision, even modest steps can reclaim agency over a life too often dictated by habit and obligation.

Once her clients grasp what they truly want, Allison guides them to root out what they've been fleeing. Any pattern of job-hopping, relationship cycling, or serial side-projects can usually be traced to a single unaddressed wound. Unless that wound is faced—unpacked and understood—it resurfaces endlessly in new contexts. As Allison asks, if you are running away, what exactly are you escaping, and how might you heal it so that you can finally run toward something that feels both purposeful and aligned?

Her own career arc illustrates how coaching skills evolved naturally from a lifetime of leadership. A high-school salesperson of new homes learned early how to guide families through one of their largest life investments. An MBA graduate turned corporate manager discovered that every boardroom presentation, every budget negotiation, was really a lesson in human motivation and communication. By listing every past role—back to her first post-college job—and noting what brought her joy versus what drained her energy, Allison uncovered a thread that led her unerringly to coaching: a passion for helping people navigate complexity and design lives of their own choosing.

That realization soft-landed her next transition. Building on decades of experience as both a business leader and a lay-therapist of sorts, she formalized her practice, blending tactical frameworks with deep emotional inquiry. She found that clients who succeed most spectacularly are those who allow themselves to acknowledge fear, grief, or anger—then use those emotions as springboards rather than shackles.

Throughout her evolution, Allison benefited from her own mentors. She credits one executive coach from ten years ago with teaching her to remove emotion from strategic decisions and to reclaim personal power. That mentor's influence not only guided Allison through her toughest professional chapter but also inspired her to train under the International Coach Federation, bringing a rigorous certification to her heartfelt approach.

Today, Allison measures success not by the size of her clientele, but by the small intentions she helps clients set and achieve. She shuns rigid SMART goals in favor of flexible intentions— little commitments that honor each person's humanity and evolve with life's ebbs and flows. Her own intention for this year is deceptively modest: to master eleven push-ups, a concrete symbol of regained strength and resilience. It speaks to her belief that even the tiniest victories can reignite momentum and self-belief.

In Volume 3 of The Inspired Choice Chronicles—Built to Give— Allison's story exemplifies how leading with generosity transforms both individual lives and the organizations they inhabit. By first giving herself the permission to pause, reflect, and heal, she gained the clarity to offer her clients far more than career advice—she offers them the gift of alignment. And in doing so, she sparks a ripple effect: every person who learns to run toward purpose rather than away from pain brings that power back into their families, teams, and communities.

Allison's journey reminds us that the greatest changes often begin not with grand gestures, but with the courage to face our own whispers of discontent, to set intentions no matter how small, and to trust that we are indeed built to give—first to ourselves, and then to the world.

Season 13, Episode 1, aired 4/23/2025

recorded 4/16/2025 Flower Mound, TX, US / Lisbon, Portugal

Connect with Allison: http://www.hall-williams.com/

5. GIVING AS A STRATEGY: BUILDING BUSINESSES THAT SERVE

Giving as a strategy is not just about philanthropy or corporate responsibility initiatives. It is about embedding contribution into the very core of your business model. Organizations that integrate giving into their DNA not only create greater social impact but also position themselves for lasting success. In today's economy, consumers, employees, and partners are increasingly drawn to companies that stand for something meaningful. It is no longer enough to have a good product or service; people want to support businesses that reflect their values and make a positive difference in the world. Building a business that serves begins with asking different questions. Instead of focusing solely on profit margins and market share, you ask: How can we solve real problems? How can we uplift the communities we operate in? How can we contribute to something bigger than ourselves while still achieving financial sustainability? It is a shift in mindset from extraction to contribution, from short-term wins to long-term value creation. When you build around service, you foster deeper loyalty from your customers, inspire greater commitment from your team, and build a reputation that marketing budgets alone could never buy. The changemakers in this book didn't just bolt giving onto the side of their businesses like an afterthought. They made service part of their core offering. Whether by mentoring others, reinvesting profits into community projects, offering educational programs, or structuring products to create social benefit, they designed businesses that amplified their impact at every level. Giving was not a side project; it was a strategic choice that strengthened their growth and resilience. Embedding giving into your strategy doesn't have to be complicated. It can start small. It can be a percentage of profits donated to aligned causes. It can be dedicating employee time to volunteer projects. It can be creating programs that offer mentorship, training, or opportunity to those who might otherwise be left behind. The key is authenticity. Giving needs to be aligned with your mission and your values, not just a marketing campaign. People can sense when service is genuine—and when it is not. There is also an important internal effect. When giving becomes part of your business culture, it transforms your organization from the inside out. Employees feel greater purpose in their work. Leaders make decisions with a broader lens. Collaboration increases. Turnover decreases. Innovation flourishes because people are connected to a bigger why. Service becomes the heartbeat of the company, fueling not just better results, but better lives. You might wonder: will focusing on giving detract from profitability? In fact, the opposite is often true. Studies show that companies with strong social impact initiatives outperform their peers over the long term. They attract more loyal customers, more committed employees, and more meaningful partnerships. Their brand equity strengthens. Their communities become allies rather than bystanders. Financial health and social good are not opposing forces. When approached wisely, they amplify each other. The beautiful truth is this: giving is good business. It is not a distraction. It is not a luxury reserved for billionaires. It is a strategy available to you right now, at whatever stage you are in. You do not need to wait until you have reached some imagined milestone. You can start weaving service into your operations today. Every action you take from a spirit of contribution builds momentum. Every decision that considers the broader impact adds to your legacy.

The most enduring businesses are those that give more than they take. They serve not because they have to, but because they know it is the right way to build something that matters. You have the power to be one of those leaders. You have the opportunity to build one of those businesses. Giving is not just an act of kindness. It is a courageous, strategic, and inspired choice that multiplies value in ways you may never fully see but will always deeply feel. Start now. Build to give. Grow to serve.

6. THE POWER OF STORY: SHARING YOUR MISSION WITH THE WORLD

Stories have always been the way we understand ourselves, each other, and the world. Long before data, before marketing campaigns, before social media, it was stories that moved hearts and inspired action. And in today's noisy, fast-paced world, story remains the most powerful tool you have to connect your mission with the people who need it most. When you share your story authentically, you are not just communicating information. You are building trust. You are inviting people into your journey. You are showing them not just what you do, but why you do it, and why it matters. Facts inform. Stories transform. They turn passive listeners into active participants in your mission. For entrepreneurs and changemakers who are building organizations rooted in giving, storytelling is not optional. It is essential. Your story brings your mission to life. It makes your vision tangible. It allows people to see themselves in the future you are working to create. Whether you are seeking donors, customers, partners, or volunteers, it is your story that will inspire them to believe, to care, and to act. But powerful storytelling is not about exaggeration or manipulation. It is about truth, vulnerability, and clarity. It is about owning your journey—the struggles, the turning points, the lessons learned. It is about sharing the moments that defined your mission and the impact you are striving to create. Authenticity always wins. People are drawn to realness, not perfection. When crafting and sharing your story, start with your why. What first moved you to act? What injustice, need, or opportunity opened your eyes and stirred your heart? Paint that picture. Help your audience feel what you felt. Then, share your vision. What are you working toward? What change do you want to see in the world? What future are you helping to build? Be bold. Big visions ignite big support. Next, connect the dots. Show how your mission and your audience's values align. Help them see that by supporting your work—whether through donations, collaboration, or simply spreading the word—they are becoming part of the story too. People want to belong to something bigger than themselves.

Your story gives them that chance. Remember, the hero of your story is not just you. It is your mission, your community, the people you serve, and the people who join you along the way. Good storytelling focuses less on "look at me" and more on "look at what we can do together." It invites shared ownership of the vision. Today, you have more tools than ever to share your story widely. Podcasts, videos, blogs, social media, speaking engagements—each platform offers an opportunity to reach hearts and minds. But no matter the medium, the message must stay true. Speak from the heart. Share specific, vivid moments. Highlight real people and real impact. Be consistent. A story told once is interesting; a story told consistently becomes a movement. As you build your organization and expand your impact, never underestimate the power of narrative. A powerful story can open doors that logic and credentials cannot. It can rally support, attract champions, and transform skeptics into believers. It can sustain momentum when times are hard and amplify your reach when opportunities arise. You are already living a story worth telling. Every risk you have taken, every challenge you have overcome, every life you have touched—they are all part of the narrative unfolding around you. You do not need to invent something impressive. You only need to share the journey honestly, with courage and care.

In a world where people are inundated with noise, authenticity cuts through. Purpose speaks louder than polish. Heart resonates deeper than hype. Let your story be the bridge that connects your mission to the people it is meant to serve.

Your voice matters. Your vision matters. Your journey matters. Tell your story. Share your mission. Inspire the world.

Building something meaningful is never a solo act. No matter how talented, driven, or visionary you are, your impact multiplies when you collaborate with others who share your commitment to making a difference. Partnerships are the lifeblood of sustainable, scalable change. They allow you to combine strengths, extend your reach, and create outcomes that no single individual or organization could achieve alone. At its best, collaboration is not about compromise; it is about synergy. It is not about giving up your vision but expanding it through the collective power of aligned efforts. The most effective partnerships are rooted in shared values, mutual respect, and a genuine belief in the mission. They are not just transactional agreements. They are relationships built on trust and a common purpose. When you are building a business, a nonprofit, or a movement, seeking out the right partners can accelerate your progress in extraordinary ways. Strategic partnerships can provide access to new audiences, new resources, and new capabilities. They can help you overcome limitations, fill gaps in expertise, and amplify your message across broader platforms. They bring fresh perspectives that challenge you to grow and innovate. But not all partnerships are created equal. Successful collaboration requires discernment. It is essential to align not just on goals, but on deeper questions of approach, philosophy, and culture. A flashy partnership that looks good on paper but misaligns on core values will ultimately erode your mission rather than strengthen it. Take the time to choose partners who genuinely care about the people you serve and who share your commitment to long-term impact over short-term gain. Communication is the foundation of every strong partnership. Be clear about your vision, your needs, and your expectations from the start. Listen deeply to your partners as well. What are their hopes, challenges, and measures of success? Build agreements that honor the contributions of everyone involved. Approach collaboration as a relationship to be nurtured, not a transaction to be completed. Flexibility is another crucial ingredient. Every partnership will face challenges—different working styles, shifting circumstances, unexpected obstacles. The willingness to adapt, to problem-solve together, and to stay focused on the shared mission is what will carry your partnership through the inevitable rough patches. Trust grows when you show up for each other, especially when things do not go according to plan. Celebrating shared victories is just as important as weathering challenges. Take time to acknowledge milestones, big and small. Recognize the contributions of your partners publicly and privately. Gratitude fuels collaboration. People who feel seen, valued, and appreciated are far more likely to continue giving their best energy to the partnership. Sometimes, partnerships will be long-term alliances that grow and evolve alongside your organization. Other times, they will be temporary collaborations focused on a specific project or campaign. Both types are valuable. The key is to be intentional about building relationships, not just extracting benefits. The changemakers you meet throughout this book did not succeed alone. They built ecosystems of support. They fostered alliances with other nonprofits, businesses, mentors, sponsors, volunteers, and community leaders. They understood that giving back at scale requires weaving a web of interconnected impact, each strand strengthening the others. If you want to maximize your impact, start thinking beyond your immediate circle. Who shares your passion for the cause you champion? Who has complementary skills or resources? Who would be energized to join forces with you to create something bigger than either of you could do alone? Reach out. Start the conversation. Plant the seeds. Collaboration is not a sign of weakness. It is a strategy of wisdom. It is a recognition that we are stronger together than we could ever be apart. When you build partnerships that matter, you are not just adding resources—you are multiplying possibility. The future belongs to those who build bridges, not walls. To those who understand that greatness is not measured by how much you can achieve alone, but by how much you can create together. Partnerships are not the side road to impact. They are the main road.

Open your hand. Extend your heart. Invite others in. Together, you can move mountains.

8. FROM PODCAST TO PLATFORM: USING YOUR VOICE FOR CHANGE

Your voice is one of the most powerful tools you have to inspire, influence, and ignite change. In today's world, anyone can build a platform. You do not need permission. You do not need perfect credentials. You simply need the willingness to share your message, your mission, and your heart with the world. A podcast is more than a show. It is a platform for impact, a catalyst for community, and a bridge between ideas and action. Starting a podcast might seem like a small step. After all, it begins with one microphone, one conversation, one episode. But do not underestimate its potential. A podcast can reach thousands. It can connect you with people across continents. It can introduce you to collaborators, supporters, and future leaders who believe in the same vision you hold. It becomes a living archive of your values, your insights, and your commitment to making a difference. For mission-driven entrepreneurs and nonprofit leaders, a podcast is an extraordinary tool. It allows you to tell your story on your terms. It gives you a way to elevate the voices of others, to showcase the work happening in the communities you serve, and to inspire listeners to get involved. It builds trust through consistency and authenticity. And it positions you as a leader— not because you have all the answers, but because you are willing to create a space for important conversations. Turning a podcast into a true platform for change begins with clarity. What do you stand for? What impact do you want to create? Who are you speaking to? The more clearly you define your purpose and your audience, the more powerfully your podcast will resonate. Every episode should be an extension of your mission, a thread that weaves into the larger story you are building with your life and work. Consistency is key. Impact grows over time, not overnight. It is easy to feel like your voice is too small or that no one is listening in the beginning. But every episode you release is a seed planted. Every conversation you host is a ripple created. Trust the process. Stay aligned with your purpose, and your audience will find you.

Authenticity matters even more than polish. Listeners crave realness. They want to hear the struggles as well as the victories. They want to connect with the human behind the mission. When you show up with honesty, vulnerability, and genuine passion, you create a bond that transcends marketing. You build a community, not just a following. A podcast is also a springboard for greater opportunities. It can lead to speaking engagements, partnerships, book deals, and expanded visibility for your cause. It positions you as a trusted voice in your field. It opens doors you may not even know exist yet. Every conversation recorded is a conversation that might change someone's life. But beyond the metrics and milestones, remember this: if even one listener is inspired to take action because of something they heard on your show, you have already made a difference. One voice can light a spark that travels farther than you will ever see. Do not wait for the perfect moment to start. Do not wait until you feel ready or flawless. The world needs your voice now. It needs your perspective, your story, your hope. Start where you are, with what you have, and trust that it will grow. Your podcast can be more than a project. It can be a platform for service, connection, and transformation. It can be a lighthouse for those seeking direction. It can be a celebration of the everyday heroes and changemakers who are quietly building a better world.

Use your voice. Share your mission. Build your platform—not for fame or fortune, but for impact. The microphone is in your hands. What will you say? Who will you inspire? What movement will you spark?

Your voice matters. Speak your truth. Serve through your platform. Change starts with a conversation—and the next one could start with you.

9. START WHERE YOU ARE: SMALL ACTS, BIG RESULTS

One of the greatest myths about making an impact is that you have to wait. Wait until you have more experience. Wait until you have more money. Wait until the timing is perfect. But real change is never built on waiting. It is built on starting—right where you are, with exactly what you have. You do not need a massive platform, a multimillion-dollar budget, or a decade of expertise to make a difference. You need a willing heart, a clear intention, and the courage to act. Every great movement, every transformative project, every wave of change began with a small, seemingly ordinary action. A conversation. A donation. A decision to care. Starting small does not mean thinking small. It means honoring the power of momentum. When you take one small step, you create a ripple that leads to another, and another. Over time, those small actions add up to big results. A book gets written one word at a time. A business gets built one relationship at a time. A community gets transformed one act of service at a time. Too often, we talk ourselves out of action because we believe our effort will not be enough. But impact is not about size. It is about intention. It is about consistency. It is about showing up when it would be easier to stay comfortable. When you start where you are, you signal to the universe—and to yourself— that you are serious about making a difference. You have more to offer than you realize. Your skills, your experiences, your passions, your connections—each of these is a resource that can be leveraged for good. Look around your life. Where is there a need you can meet? Where is there a person you can support, a cause you can champion, a conversation you can start? The opportunities for contribution are everywhere. We simply have to be willing to see them. Starting where you are also means starting with who you are. You do not have to become someone else to be of service. You do not have to wait until you are "better," "smarter," or "more successful." Your current self is enough. Your journey, with all its imperfections and learning curves, is exactly what equips you to help someone else take the next step on theirs.

Sometimes, the first step is simply saying yes. Yes to volunteering an hour. Yes to mentoring one person. Yes to donating a skill you take for granted. Yes to starting that passion project you have been putting off. Yes to reaching out and offering your hand when someone needs it most. And yes, sometimes starting small feels vulnerable. It requires humility to offer what you have without knowing how it will be received. It requires trust to believe that your contribution matters even when the results are not immediately visible. But trust it anyway. Trust that every seed you plant will grow in ways you cannot yet see. The changemakers in this book did not wait for ideal conditions. They started. They served. They built, one choice at a time. Their impact is a testament to the power of small beginnings fueled by big commitment. You have the same potential. You have the same opportunity. You have the same invitation. The world does not need you to be perfect. It needs you to be present. It needs you to care enough to act. It needs you to believe that your small act could be the beginning of something extraordinary.

Start where you are. Use what you have. Do what you can. And trust that it is enough to begin.

Big results are not reserved for the powerful or the privileged. They are created by people who are willing to take small, courageous steps every day. People like you.

Today, you have a choice. You can wait for the perfect moment—or you can decide that this moment is enough. The future is shaped by those who dare to start.

At the core of every life well lived is the simple truth that we are built to give. We are wired for connection, for contribution, for creating something that extends beyond ourselves. When you embrace this truth, you stop measuring success only by what you accumulate and start measuring it by what you leave behind. Your legacy is not something you build at the end of your life. It is something you build every day, through every choice, every relationship, every act of generosity. Legacy is not about monuments or medals. It is about impact. It is about the lives you touch, the values you embody, the changes you set in motion. It is about the ripples you create that continue long after you are gone. True legacy is not an afterthought. It is the natural result of living with intention, with courage, and with a heart committed to service. When you recognize that you are built to give, everything changes. Work becomes more than a paycheck. It becomes a platform for impact. Leadership becomes more than authority. It becomes stewardship of potential. Wealth becomes more than accumulation. It becomes a tool for empowerment. Every area of your life becomes an opportunity to invest in something bigger than yourself. You do not have to wait until you reach a certain level of success to start building your legacy. You are building it now. In the way you treat people. In the causes you champion. In the way you show up when it would be easier not to. Every interaction is a brick in the foundation of the future you are creating. Living with a legacy mindset also brings clarity. It helps you discern where to spend your energy, your time, your resources. It pushes you to focus on what truly matters and to let go of what does not. It reminds you that your worth is not measured by your titles or your possessions but by the difference you make in the lives of others. Building your legacy starts with a simple but powerful decision: to live with purpose. To choose contribution over complacency. To choose impact over convenience. To choose courage over comfort. Every day offers new chances to align your actions with your higher values. Every moment is an opportunity to plant seeds that will bear fruit far beyond your immediate reach.

You may never see the full extent of the difference you make. You may never know all the lives you touch or the hearts you inspire. But trust that the impact is real. Trust that your choices today will echo into tomorrow and beyond. The most powerful legacies are built quietly, steadily, by people who simply refuse to leave the world the way they found it. As you move forward from reading this book, ask yourself: What do I want my legacy to be? What am I willing to build, to sacrifice, to invest, in order to leave that legacy behind? What choices can I make today that my future self—and future generations—will thank me for? You are built to give. You are built to lift others, to spark hope, to create possibility. You are built to create beauty, healing, and change. Your gifts, your story, your heart—they are needed now more than ever.

Let your life be a living testament to the power of giving. Let your legacy be one of light, strength, and generosity. Let your journey inspire others to believe that they too are built to give— and that by doing so, they can change the world.

You do not have to be perfect to leave a legacy. You just have to be willing. Willing to care. Willing to show up. Willing to give.

Your legacy is already in motion. Build it with love. Build it with courage. Build it with the unwavering belief that your life, your work, and your choices can make a lasting difference.

You are built to give. Now go build the future that only you can create.

11. A HEARTFELT THANK YOU

Every journey worth taking is filled with moments of gratitude. As this book comes to a close, I want to pause and say thank you—to you, the reader, for choosing to spend your precious time with these stories, these ideas, and this vision. Your willingness to explore what it means to build a life and a business based on giving is itself an act of courage.

Thank you to the extraordinary guests who shared their defining moments and inspired so much of what you've read here. Your generosity of spirit, your vulnerability, and your dedication to service continue to ripple outward in ways you may never fully see. You are proof that impact is made choice by choice, heart by heart.

Thank you to every mentor, teacher, friend, and fellow traveler who has shown me that giving is not a sacrifice, but a joy. That service is not an obligation, but an opportunity. And that true success is measured not by what we hold onto, but by what we are willing to share.

Thank you to the incredible community around The Inspired Choice. Your belief in choosing differently, in living purposefully, and in serving generously is what makes all of this possible. You are not just readers—you are changemakers. You are the living proof that inspired choices can transform lives, businesses, and entire communities.

Finally, thank you to every person out there who dares to believe that their one life can make a difference. You are the heartbeat of this book. You are the reason this work matters.

Never underestimate the power of your voice, your gifts, and your willingness to give. The world needs what only you can bring. Thank you for being part of this movement. Thank you for being built to give.

12. ABOUT CAROLINE

Caroline Biesalski is a coach, speaker, podcast host, and founder of The Inspired Choice Foundation. Through her work, she empowers entrepreneurs, creatives, and purpose-driven leaders to make courageous choices that align with their deepest values and highest vision.

With a background that bridges business strategy, communication, and personal transformation, Caroline helps individuals turn inspired ideas into sustainable action. She is passionate about creating spaces where people can connect, grow, and build lasting impact.

The Inspired Choice Chronicles series was born from her belief that every choice matters—and that through intentional giving, we can build lives, businesses, and legacies that change the world for the better.

Caroline lives and works internationally, continuing to explore how creativity, service, and entrepreneurship come together to fuel lasting change.

Connect with Caroline through The Inspired Choice Foundation or join her on The Inspired Choice Podcast for ongoing inspiration, practical tools, and powerful conversations about making your mark through giving.

IT'S YOUR CHOICE

The Inspired Choice Chronicles have always been built around a simple but powerful truth: you are one choice away from a new future.

This volume, Built to Give, invites you to take that truth even deeper. To realize that giving is not something you do after you succeed—it is how you succeed. It is not an extra; it is the essence. It is not reserved for the few; it is available to all of us.

Right now, you have a choice.
You can choose to see your gifts, your work, and your voice as tools for impact.
You can choose to plant seeds of hope, empowerment, and possibility wherever you go.
You can choose to build your life, your business, and your legacy on a foundation of service.

The size of the act does not matter. The size of the heart behind it does.

Start where you are. Give what you can. Trust that it matters more than you know.

You were built to give. You were built to create change. You were built to leave a legacy of courage, compassion, and contribution.

The next chapter is yours to write.
The next inspired choice is yours to make.

Choose boldly.
Choose generously.
Choose to give.

Authentic Stories, Surprising Lessons, and Practical Takeaways for Podcast or Business Starters empowering you to make impactful choices for both your personal and professional life.

Listen to The Inspired Choice podcast

www.podcast.inspiredchoice.today

Choose your platform: Apple Podcasts, Spotify, YouTube

Use the AI Chat to get answers about guests and topics

Become an inspiring interview guest by applying here

https://www.podmatch.com/hostdetailpreview/inspiredchoice

or send an E-Mail to interview@inspiredchoice.today

for any requests, feedback or further information about THE INSPIRED CHOICE Mentoring with Caroline Biesalski

See you in the next adventurous chapter of your life!

Yours,
Caroline Biesalski
The Inspired Choice Foundation